REMARKS
ON
RIFLE GUNS

by
EZEKIEL BAKER

The Naval & Military Press Ltd

Published by
The Naval & Military Press Ltd
Unit 10 Ridgewood Industrial Park,
Uckfield, East Sussex,
TN22 5QE England
Tel: +44 (0) 1825 749494
Fax: +44 (0) 1825 765701
www.naval-military-press.com

In reprinting in facsimile from the original, any imperfections are inevitably reproduced and the quality may fall short of modern type and cartographic standards.

BAKER'S REMARKS,

WITH

SUPPLEMENT.

1823.

REMARKS

ON

RIFLE GUNS;

being the result of

FORTY YEARS PRACTICE AND OBSERVATIONS:

with

SPECIFIC REMARKS

ON FOWLING PIECES.

Eighth Edition,

WITH CONSIDERABLE ADDITIONS AND IMPROVEMENTS.

To which is added,

A SUPPLEMENT,

Respecting an Additional Improvement

IN GUN AND DOOR LOCKS, AND SPRING BOLTS;

for which

A THIRD SILVER MEDAL HAS BEEN AWARDED BY THE

SOCIETY OF ARTS:

containing

A DESCRIPTION OF A NEW MACHINE

FOR TAKING TRUE SIGHT IN SHOOTING FLYING, AND IMPORTANT REMARKS ON THE

PERCUSSION LOCK.

➤➤◄◄

By EZEKIEL BAKER,

GUN AND RIFLE MAKER TO HIS MAJESTY GEORGE THE FOURTH, *The Hon. Board of Ordnance, and the Hon. East India Company.*

DEDICATED,

BY PERMISSION, TO HIS MOST GRACIOUS MAJESTY,

King George the Fourth.

DEDICATED,

BY PERMISSION,

TO THE KING.

SIRE,

In presuming to solicit Your Majesty's gracious permission to honor this Eighth Edition of my Work with Your Majesty's most illustrious Name, I was buoyed up with the hope, that the suggestions therein contained on the bursting of gun-barrels, operating for the preservation of the lives of Your Majesty's Subjects, would atone for whatever deficiency might be found in this Volume, by a Sovereign, whose feelings are so alive to the welfare of His

DEDICATION.

People, and whose judgment so correctly appreciates the value of scientific works.

With reverence and gratitude, SIRE, and with the most devoted attachment,

I have the honor to subscribe myself,

YOUR MAJESTY'S

Very Loyal and Dutiful

Subject and Servant,

EZEKIEL BAKER.

June, 1821.

CONTENTS.

	PAGE
INTRODUCTION	1
OF LOADING	5
OF PRESENTING AND TAKING AIM	28
OF JUDGING DISTANCES	38
GENERAL OBSERVATIONS	42
AN EXPERIMENT	76
DITTO	82
OF PROVING AND RE-PROVING BARRELS	84
OF CASTING BALLS	91
OF THE BULLET MOULD	95
SPECIFIC REMARKS ON FOWLING PIECES	106
OF BURSTING OF BLUNDERBUSSES	123
CONCLUSION	127

RIFLEMAN PRESENTING

Published by E. Baker Gun maker No 24 White Chapel Road opposite the Church from Little Alie Street.

No 1.

RIFLEMAN PRESENTING

No. 4.

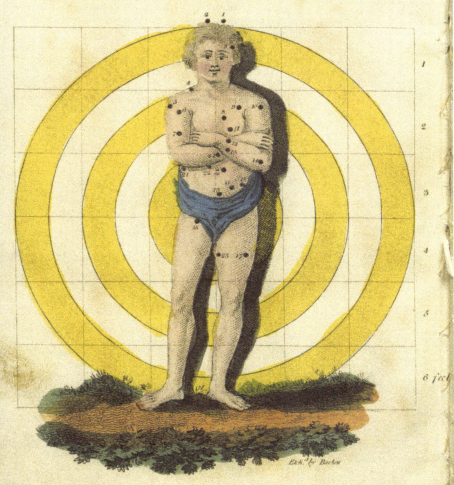

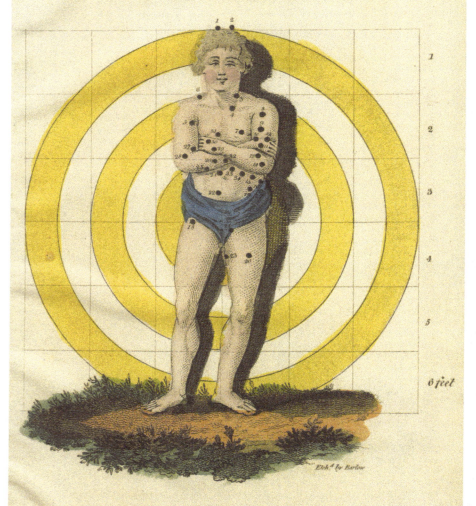

INTRODUCTION.

In presenting an EIGHTH EDITION of this Work to the Public, I should be wanting in gratitude not to acknowledge the liberal and extensive patronage which it has received: at the same time, I cannot but feel proud that my labors in the public service have been distinguished by the approbation of Exalted Rank, and by the consciousness that my exertions have tended, in a great degree, to prevent the numerous accidents which so repeatedly occurred, before I had the honor of giving publicity to a PRACTICAL EXPERIENCE of forty years.

INTRODUCTION.

During this long period, I have devoted all my time, I have exerted all my energies, in furtherance of the great object I had in view—that of averting the evils which arise from the bursting of barrels; and I have also endeavored to point out the best means, and to give every information relative to the use, and I may add the abuse, of rifles, guns, pistols, &c.

In a work of this nature, it is almost impossible to avoid occasional repetition, as the explanation of one part necessarily calls the attention to every other attached to it: but I conceive it at all times much better " to say *that* twice, than not to say it all;" and I would rather have the imputation

INTRODUCTION. 3

of being minutely verbose, than not be sufficiently explicit where the lives of my fellow-creatures are at stake.

I am not ambitious to be ranked among the literati; but I confess I am most anxious to avert danger, and to give every publicity to opinions which are founded on PRACTICE—at the same time I have THEORETICALLY endeavored to give importance to a subject which has been too long neglected.

In this Edition, I have arranged the various subjects treated of under separate and distinct heads, so that the reader may easily refer to specific divisions. I have also made some important additions; more particularly " The

INTRODUCTION.

Weight and Diameter of Lead Balls cast from various moulds, and divided into distinct parts of an inch," &c. with a description of a newly-invented BULLET-MOULD AND CLIPPER ; and " Specific Remarks on Fowling Pieces;" —and I trust that the candor of the Public will duly appreciate the purity of my intentions.

REMARKS.

OF LOADING.

In apportioning the quantity of powder for a rifle, one charge for all distances should be carefully attended to; and if the powder be good, I have ascertained that nearly one third of the weight of the ball, priming included, is the best estimate. After you have loaded the piece with powder, then put the greased patch of leather, calico, or soft rag, provided for that purpose, on the end of the barrel, as near the centre as possible; place the ball upon it with the neck or castable, where it is cut off from

6 OF LOADING.

the moulds, downwards, as generally there is a small hole or cavity in it, which would gather the air in its flight;* but if this plan be adopted, and the smooth side always kept upwards in the barrel, it will not be so liable to be obstructed in its passage through the atmosphere.

Great care should also be taken that the ball is in the middle of the patch of leather or greased rag, before it is rammed down the barrel: if it is more on one side than the other, it will give the ball an inclination, and throw it from the straight line on its leaving the barrel. Both sides of the patch should be greased; in which case there can be no

* By my newly-invented Bullet-mould, as described hereafter, this imperfection is entirely removed.

OF LOADING. 7

mistake, however hurried you may be in loading. I have tried various ways of loading rifles at the breech, by means of screws placed in different positions; but, after a few rounds firing, the screws have become so clogged by the filth from the powder working round them, as to become very difficult to move, and will in time be eaten away with rust, which will render them dangerous to use; none answer the general purpose better than those loaded at the muzzle, with the patches as above-mentioned: by which method, the grooves of the rifle become air-tight; the filth from the powder is carried down upon the charge; and the barrel is preserved clean, much more so, indeed, with the quarter turn, than it would with the whole one, or three-quarter turn. In rifle, I have occasion-

8 OF LOADING.

ally fired naked balls without patches, that have filled up the grooves; but after a few rounds firing, I have found it very difficult to load; and, consequently, the patch is by far the most advantageous method.

A ball should never be forced down too hard, nor yet should it be too easy; I never found them to go so true, as when they properly fitted. The ball with its patch should fit air-tight, or it will not have the desired effect. Let the rifle be ever so well cut, if the ball does not fit, it will not answer the intended purpose. I do not mean that the ball should fit so tight as to require a wooden mallet to drive it in the nose end of the barrel. When the 95th rifle regiment was raised by Government,

OF LOADING.

9

which is now called the Rifle Brigades, I supplied them with a few hundreds of small wooden mallets to drive in the ball; but they found them very inconvenient, and very soon dispensed with them: in addition to which they became a serious incumbrance to the men, and have for some years past been entirely abandoned. The loading is indeed performed equally well without them, as a man's strength is always found sufficient to make the ball enter, when it fits as it ought to do; but if, in any case, more strength should be required, I would certainly prefer wooden mallets to the rammer head, or any thing hard being made use of. I have seen many an excellent rifle barrel much injured by being bruised and cut at the nose end by the rammer

10 OF LOADING.

head, and which has consequently much impeded their accuracy of shooting.

I have fired balls of various shapes, but none to answer so well as the round ones, the rounder the better; as all parts will have a more equal bearing on the rifle. I have very little opinion of the balls for loading rifles having leather, or any other substance pasted on them as a substitute for a patch, particularly for long ranges; for in their flight they gather the air, and make a noise similar to a humming-top, which most certainly impedes their progress, and necessarily alters or changes the direction.

A barrel, from frequent using and cleansing, will sometimes become too

OF LOADING.   11

wide for the ball which first fitted it: in this case a double or treble patch should be added, according to circumstances; by which means the ball will be made to fit, and will be found to answer the purpose very well, particularly as bullet-moulds cannot at all times be got, and are also expensive. Be careful that the ball is rammed home to the powder, and with as little bruising as possible.

Every rifleman should mark his rammer at the muzzle end of the barrel, when loaded, which will shew him when the ball is close down on the powder. After firing a few rounds, the filth from the powder will clog at the bottom of the barrel, and prevent the ball from going close on the powder; in this case,

12 OF LOADING.

a little pressing with the rammer will be required to get the ball into its right place. More accidents happen from a neglect of this precaution, than can be imagined: if the ball be not rammed close on the powder, the intervening air will frequently cause the barrel to burst; not, I confess, that there is so much danger with rifle barrels, as with fowling-pieces, the former being made much stronger: but exclusive of any danger, it is an absolute requisite to insure a true flight of the ball; as no piece will carry perfect, unless this method be strictly adhered to. When the rammer is marked, as before-mentioned, it will shew when the ball is close rammed to the powder; and if, by mistake, he should load his rifle twice, the error would instantly be detected.

OF LOADING. 13

If the ball fits air-tight, as it should do, it will require two or three pushes with the rammer before the air can escape, to get it in its proper place. I do not recommend the ball, as I have before-mentioned, to be bruised with the rammer, but pushed. If the ball has ragged edges, it will be much impeded, as well as thrown from its true direction by the air, more so than when in its globular shape, in the front part of the ball. As to ramming hard on the powder, or breaking the grains, I never found it to diminish its strength, but it will frequently cause the piece to hang fire.

At all times care should be taken that the hammer is shut down upon the pan before the ball is rammed down, or

14 OF LOADING.

the air which the ball forces before it will blow all the powder out at the touch-hole. If this should occur, the ball must be drawn out with a screw turned into the end of the rammer, provided for that purpose. I do not recommend touch-holes being too small, as that will make the rifles hang fire, or flash in the pan: the touch-holes, it is true, will get wider from frequent firing, like all other guns; but that would be giving an enemy too great an advantage by our rifles missing fire, or flashing in the pan, as it would require some thousands of rounds fired, before the touch-holes would be blown too wide for the service. When that is the case, it can be screwed or bushed up with an iron pin, and another hole drilled in by the

OF LOADING. 15

armourers of the regiments at a small expense, when it will be equal as when first new; and the diameter of which should be nearly the sixteenth part of an inch. Whenever the barrel is cleaned, it is necessary that the touch-hole should be well cleared with a small feather, a piece of rag, or tow, pushed through it with a small wire or touch-hole pricker, until dry, which will preserve it for many years: it is also necessary to sponge out and clean the rifle-piece after practice. If it is sponged out often whilst firing, it will be all the better, should there be time, as a rifle cannot be kept too clean. After firing ten or twelve rounds, I have found the ball ramble from the point intended; and sponging out the barrel will have the effect of preventing such

16 OF LOADING.

an occurrence. The wash-eye that screws in the end of the ramrod should be kept in the box that is in the stock of the rifle, with oiled rag, or tow, in it, to be at all times ready to sponge out the barrel during the time of firing. Under the head of the rammer is a small hole, to put in a lever, which makes the rammer similar to a carpenter's gimlet, and forms a purchase to screw into the ball, and by that means the ball is easily drawn out of the barrel: but after firing a few rounds, it will be found difficult to draw out the ball. To remedy this, I have found the following method to have the desired effect. Pour a little water down the barrel, and by working the rammer gently up and down, the filth will become

OF LOADING. 17

loosened, and the ball will be drawn with ease. It may happen that water, at such times, cannot be got: if the man can make urine, and apply it in the same kind of way, it will have the same effect. After the ball is drawn, it will adhere so fast on the screw, that the fingers cannot unscrew it; if so, lay the ball on a stone or hard ground, and strike it with the butt end of the rifle to flatten it; it will then be taken off with ease. The barrel should be wiped dry before loaded again.

The same process will be equally efficacious to loosen the ramrod in fowling-pieces, when it sticks fast in the barrel, by the wadding getting round the tip of the ramrod: I have frequently

c

OF LOADING.

experienced such an untoward circumstance, and have no doubt that thousands of sportsmen have done the same. Indeed I have known many gentlemen actually shoot away the ramrod, because they could not get it out of the barrel, which has hindered their sport for a day or two, before they could get another; this disappointment has been sensibly felt by many of the sons of the trigger; but can easily be prevented by the method I have laid down.

The pans of rifle-locks should be grooved on each side, or what is termed raised, to admit of the water and filth which will accumulate after firing a few rounds. Filth from the powder driven against the fence will keep the hammer

OF LOADING. 19

so open as to lose the prime, and all the powder will be blown out of the barrel by forcing down the ball. The locks to the rifles that I have made for the Honorable East India Company are so raised; and are also inclined towards the fence that shortens the lower part of the hammer, which makes it leave the pan sooner, and admits the fire more expeditiously into the prime. The locks for muskets raised in this manner would answer very well.

The hammers of musket-locks in general play very stiff, particularly when new, insomuch that soldiers find a difficulty in shutting and opening the pan; in order to make it play easy, they endeavor to weaken it by cramping the

OF LOADING.

hammer-spring, which renders it nearly useless, as, when fired, it has not sufficient power to resist the flint to make it fire as it ought to do. This is one occasion of the lock so often missing fire, which must be a great hindrance to the service, particularly when in action with an enemy.

The hammers elevated over the flint would be of great advantage in giving facility to the opening of the pan. In this operation, however, with common locks, the soldiers often wound themselves in the thumb with the flint. This plan would entirely remove that imperfection, and the additional expense would be trifling in comparison to its advantages. It will also keep the hammer-face

OF LOADING. 21

clean from the filth of the thumb, which
the soldier often dirts by wiping out the
pan. This also is a great hindrance to
the flint drawing fire, as it strikes off
the hammer without cutting.

It is a gratification to me to learn,
that, from my suggestion, the Honorable
East India Company have adopted these
improvements to every description of fire-
arms used by them, which has a decided
advantage over the old patterns, as I am
convinced will be acknowledged by their
service in India. After priming and
loading, by waiting for some time before
I have had occasion to fire, I have frequently seen the damp and filth from the
powder on the hammer-face and flint,
more particularly when the atmosphere

OF LOADING.

is hazy; which has prevented any fire from being drawn. The skirt of a coat or jacket is very useful in wiping both, when not provided with rag or tow for that purpose, as a hammer-face cannot be kept too clean to ensure a good fire. Another cause why pieces very often miss fire, arises from the flint having sometimes a hard part which will neither nip nor break when struck against the hammer, although it will drive the hammer over, but not draw any fire at all; when this is the case, the whole of that part of the flint should be broken or nipped off; and then there will be no fear that the remaining part of the flint will be sufficiently effective; and those disappointments will be prevented which have so often been noticed by muskets failing in

OF LOADING. 23

that manner with soldiers on field days, to which I have frequently been an eye-witness, and of which I have had many examples forwarded to me. The same failing must occur when engaged in action with an enemy; which is of serious importance to the service: as, in my opinion, no situation can be so galling, no vexation can equal that of a brave fellow filling up the ranks merely to be fired at, and at the same time be disabled from doing his duty. Conscious of his inability to return the fire, he remains like an automaton, and perhaps vents condemnation against his musket, or rather the maker, when a slight attention might remove every difficulty. If the soldier should not have his turnscrew at hand, a stone, the rim of the bayonet, or the

24 OF LOADING.

rammer-head, will be equally effective in removing the impediment, and the flint will then be found to fire. These suggestions I strongly enforce on the attention of officers, well knowing their good effects, and which will save time in putting in new ones, particularly in actions when there is not sufficient time for so doing.

If the flint is not placed in a proper position to strike against the hammer, it will be an additional cause, also, of the piece missing fire. The flint should be fixed in the cock with the flat side upwards, so as to strike the hammer in a proper place to draw fire, and conduct it into the pan. If it strikes the hammer too high, it will disperse the fire about, and, consequently, little of it will go into

OF LOADING. 25

the pan; and that which does, will be so
chilled by the air, from having so far to
fall before it goes into the priming, that
it fires the powder too slow, and makes
the piece appear to hang fire: and if it
strikes the hammer too low, it will not
go over, and of course the fire cannot
go into the pan. To ascertain when the
flint is fixed in a proper position, let it
be struck over, and you will easily per-
ceive how the fire is dispersed about: if
it strikes the hammer so high as the fire
is dispersed, then lay double the lead or
leather that the flint is fixed in under the
flint against the cock, which will lower
the fore part of the flint, and cause it
to strike the hammer lower: if it strikes
too low, double the lead or leather as
before-mentioned, under the flint at the

26 OF LOADING.

fore end of the under jaw of the cock, which will raise it to a proper position to fire. As the jaws of the cocks are not all in the same position, and the flints are not all of the same thickness, nor of the same shape, a piece of paper, or any other soft substance, carefully placed under the flint at either end, as may be required according to the foregoing directions, will obviate every evil. This remedy will be found useful in the flinting of all locks, as well as muskets, &c. as much depends on the flint being put in properly for the lock to fire true and well.

That pieces frequently miss fire, when the flint is good, and the lock and hammer seem quite perfect, is undeniable

OF LOADING.

27

—and very few are aware of the real cause; for it is not always the fault of the flint, or lock, but because the hammer-faces, from frequent firing, become soft, by the flint cutting through the case-hardening. This happens sooner in some than others, which is owing to the variation of the metal, although of the same temperature: to prevent the possibility of a disappointment in this respect, I would recommend two hammers to all military locks, particularly to the rifle, which is more fired with than any other. When one hammer becomes soft from use, the other can be substituted, and the armorer will have time to re-harden the former: indeed, it is one of his principal duties to see that the hammers and springs are of a proper temper for the locks to fire.

PRESENTING AND TAKING AIM.

No noise or conversation should take place whilst any one is presenting or taking aim, as it will arrest the attention. The rifle should be held firm in hand, in all positions, in presenting to fire, as a great deal depends on the true flight and strength of the ball, by the rifle being kept tight to the shoulder whilst firing.

I have found, by experience, that the swell of wood, underneath the stock, similar to a pistol, has a much better

OF PRESENTING. 29

purchase to the trigger-hand than the steel or brass scroll-guard, which is usually attached to guns of every description: it prevents the piece from recoiling, and, by holding it firm to the shoulder, gives a precision to the sight, which is peculiarly advantageous, as well to riflemen as sportsmen in general. This improvement is considered so great, that the 10th regiment of Hussars have had all their rifles constructed on this principle.

In lying on the belly, it will be found difficult for the left hand to grasp the stock forward; in that case, the sling or belt should be pulled firmly back, to keep the rifle steady whilst firing, as appears in figures presenting, Nos. 2 and

30 OF PRESENTING AND

3. To fire off-hand without a rest, the right foot should be behind the left about sixteen inches, the left knee upright and not bent, the right elbow down towards the body, the butt of the rifle in the hollow of the shoulder, the body easily bent forwards, so that the right eye comes over the great toe of the left foot, as figure presenting, No. 1.—I have seen some positions of riflemen with part of the butt of the rifle appearing above the shoulder, and the remaining part of the butt upon the joint of the arm, instead of the hollow of the shoulder.

After firing a few rounds it becomes very unpleasant to the arm to receive the recoil from the rifle, instead of the shoulder. This is one reason that complaint

TAKING AIM. 31

is so often made of guns recoiling. Every one that is in the habit of shooting endeavors to put the butt in the hollow of his shoulder, to bring it as near to the centre of his body as possible, in order to prevent shooting across, which is often imperceptibly done, and which excites the wonder of the practitioner that he is so far from striking the object he aims at; this has frequently occurred to me, particularly when in a hurry to fire. I have found quarter-face the strongest position, as a piece cannot be held too firm in hand whilst presenting and firing; and besides, the man is less exposed to his enemy in that situation, than in full face, as figure presenting, No. 1.

If the body is more bent, the man

32 OF PRESENTING AND

will neither stand so easy nor so steady. The left hand, when presenting, should be forward on the swell of the stock, so as to keep the piece from dropping at the fore end, which is the case with all rifle pieces, and muskets in particular, after firing a few rounds: both pieces being heavy forwards, the left hand should be forward up the stock as far as it can be extended, so as to preserve a proper equilibrium. If the left hand is placed against the guard or handle that is in the gun in the same position that is generally used in fowling-pieces, they will depress at the fore end, and throw the ball down; the sling under the elbow, will keep it firm and steady to the shoulder, as figure presenting No. 1.

TAKING AIM. 33

In presenting and taking aim, it is far preferable to open both eyes, as the object is sooner attained, and the sight more perfect: it also prevents that blinking which is a general case in shutting one eye. This may be difficult to many at first; but " practice makes perfect:" and when it is once accomplished, the advantages will be sufficiently evident. From my former observations many persons have tried the experiment, and have since declared, that, having accustomed themselves to keep both eyes open in taking aim, they are satisfied that this method is the best, and that in every instance it has had the desired effect. By this means he will quarter his piece, which will shew him when his head is too far over the centre of the stock. The

34 OF PRESENTING AND

cheek should be pressed on the stock very hard at all times, or a man will deceive himself, for his eye should be as a fixture on the stock every time he takes aim.

In taking aim, he should place the muzzle of the rifle to the lowest part of the object he means to strike, then raise it gradually till he gets a full view of the object. In bringing up the rifle, the fore-finger must be kept light on the trigger; and when up to the point intended, he should draw the front sight into the notch of the back sight with his eye, as line drawn figure No. 4. He should hold his breath, and pull gradually without any snatching or starting, as that will materially alter the

TAKING AIM. 35

direction of the rifle. It occasionally happens that he may hold his breath so long, as to cause a trembling; in that case, the rifle should be taken down, he should breathe freely, and aim again; as it is impossible to fire so true as at the first sight. It is a more certain way to bring the muzzle of the rifle up than down, where that object can be attained. In bringing the rifle up to the point intended, the cheek should be as a fixture on the stock, that, when brought to the point, it requires no alteration; but when the muzzle is brought down, it will require the face to be pressed on the stock; in that case the point will be lost, and the man much deceived. After the trigger is pulled, let the rifle be kept firm to the shoulder, till the ball

D 2

OF PRESENTING AND

strikes the target at one hundred yards: this will be known by hearing the ball strike or hit; and that will prevent any starting or throwing back the head, as is often the case in firing.

The best sportsmen recommend all learners invariably to fire at birds without shot for some time; as, by constant practice, knowing that they cannot kill, they take a steadier view of the object, and thus become confident, that, when they have got a proper sight of the bird, it is more than probable that they may "bag their game." The same practice should be adopted with the rifle. A rifleman should for some time pull the trigger, with only a wooden driver in the cock, till he can accomplish this without

TAKING AIM. 37

starting, or shaking the muzzle of his rifle, or blinking; and, by so doing, it will give him equal confidence, and a greater command of his rifle. He should then put a little loose powder in the barrel and pan of the lock, and fire it off repeatedly: this practice would be of essential service in taking off that starting or trembling which all young practitioners universally experience.

OF JUDGING DISTANCES.

A RIFLEMAN, to judge of his distance, should be in the habit of stepping his ground from one to three hundred paces, or any other distance that may be thought proper, and let him fire at any object at the distance he steps to. By this continual practice he will learn to measure the distance with his eye to a tolerable certainty; and he should practise this method in different places and in all sorts of weather, in windy weather, and, in particular, when cross winds are prevalent. I have at all times found the cross winds most difficult to fire in, as they

OF JUDGING DISTANCES. 39

blow very irregular: if the wind blows in the front, a greater degree of elevation is required, otherwise the ball will drop, from the great body of air it meets with; if it blows in the rear, so much elevation is not required. I would recommend a young rifleman, when he can fire well at two hundred yards in calm weather, to practise in windy and all sorts of rough weather. I have found it much more difficult to fire during the time of snow falling, than in rain, the air being considerably thicker; and the flakes of snow which continually fly about distract the attention and dazzle the eye. A rifleman, indeed, should practise in all weathers, by which means he will ascertain what allowance should be made from the object to be fired at, either to

40 OF JUDGING DISTANCES.

right or left, as the wind materially influences the ball at long ranges.

I have found two hundred yards the greatest range I could fire at to any certainty. At three hundred yards I have fired very well at times when the wind has been calm. At four and five hundred yards I have frequently fired, and I have sometimes struck the object; though, having aimed as near as possible at the same point, I have found it to vary very much from the object intended: whereas at two hundred yards I could have made sure of the point, or thereabouts. From my practice, I am convinced the wind has great power on the ball, after it has passed to a certain distance. I have found it very uncertain to fire over water; and if I took

OF JUDGING DISTANCES. 41

the same elevation of the object as on land, I have found the ball drop short. Firing over swamps and bogs, has a similar effect to firing over water.

If a rifleman is in possession of a good rifle, he should never use any other until he is a complete master of the piece; after which, like the master of any other art or science, he may use any one for the information of others. I consider a person to have a perfect command of the rifle, when he can take an accurate view of the bull's eye in the target, and strike it, no matter at what distance, and take a distinct aim from any situation, whether from a right or left point, whether by elevation or depression, and insure his striking it.

ALTHOUGH I have, in the preceding divisions, given the best PRACTICAL information in my power on the first principles relating to rifles, fowling-pieces, &c. yet I feel conscious that the importance of the subject demands the most serious attention of all officers and sportsmen: —and, that the arguments which I have endeavored to enforce on their consideration may have due weight, I shall take leave to recapitulate a few

GENERAL OBSERVATIONS,

in reference to my foregoing remarks, with such additions as may arise in the

GENERAL OBSERVATIONS. 43

progress of detailing them. I repeat the maxim with which I commenced the present edition, " that it is better to say *that* twice, than not to say it at all;" and my best apology for any such repetition, is, my anxiety to do full justice to a subject which has occupied so many years of my life. It is the privilege of an old man to tell his story his own way—and, perhaps, nearly half a century devoted to one specific object may at least claim indulgence for a little tautology (if such should occur); and though the young man may smile at the garrulity of age, let them be assured, I shall feel real gratification in preserving one from the miseries arising from carelessness or ignorance, and descend to the grave with the proud consciousness of having at

44 GENERAL OBSERVATIONS.

least deserved well of my fellow-countrymen, as well as of the rising generation.

RIFLES throwing to the right or left is sometimes owing to the trigger pulling too hard, and at other times, to the man throwing his head too far over the centre of the stock. The sword or bayonet, when fixed on the barrel, will be liable to attract the sight towards it, which will give a cross sight: in taking aim, the practitioner should guard himself particularly against this, or he will be much deceived at the intended object. The sword and bayonet on fire-arms, being moved (according to patterns made by me) from the side to the under part of the barrel, in a straight line with

GENERAL OBSERVATIONS. 45

the piece, will be entirely out of the direction from attracting the eye; and will enable the soldier to charge with much greater force, and also to make more sure with his bayonet of the object he attacks. It will have the advantage of preventing the piece from being turned on the side, and the stress will be taken off his wrists, which must happen when any thing is lifted by it in the way in which bayonets are now fixed.

The alteration I have made in the false breech, at the breech-end of the barrel in rifles, by making a large deep hollow, will conduct the eye in a straight line to the sight, and will be found useful in preventing a cross sight. The impor-

46 GENERAL OBSERVATIONS.

tance of these improvements will be sufficiently obvious, and I have no doubt, when carried into practice, will meet general approbation, and be found very useful to the service in general.

By way of ascertaining whether a rifle carries to the right or left, I tried the following method, and the result of various experiments was perfectly satisfactory. I constructed a number of boards, to form a target, in a similar manner to a plate-rack. I placed twelve of these boards, half an inch thick, and separated one inch from each other, at the distance of one hundred yards, and as the ball passed, I carefully marked its direction. With a rifle which has thrown the ball from the straight line,

GENERAL OBSERVATIONS. 47

I have found it pass through the target, as above constructed, in calm weather, one inch more on one side on the outward board than the one in the centre, where the ball, from a perfect rifle, had previously entered. I have repeatedly tried this experiment, in all weathers: and am convinced that my former opinion was perfectly correct, in stating, that the wind has a powerful influence on the flight of the ball, and will cause it to fly from a straight line, even though the piece be perfectly true.

If the rifle is found to throw to the right, the back sight should be drove to the left, and the front sight to the right; both of which are left loose for that purpose; if it throws to the left, move the

48 GENERAL OBSERVATIONS.

sight contrary, as above, till the man who uses it finds it right. I do not approve of the sights being moved, after once set straight for the man that practises it.

The trigger should not draw too hard, as that will alter the direction of the rifle in firing. A rifleman, to ascertain when his trigger pulls too hard, is to suspend the trigger of the rifle on the fore-finger of his right hand, with the muzzle downwards, with the lock on full cock, (taking care the piece is not loaded, as that would be very dangerous,) which should just bear its own weight; and if it requires considerably more than the weight of the piece to pull off the trigger, it is too hard, and will take the

GENERAL OBSERVATIONS. 49

rifle out of its right direction when fired. The same rule will do to try the locks of muskets by; and the same expedient should be resorted to. I have seen many muskets where the trigger has drawn so hard as to require considerably more than their own weight to draw them off; and have often wondered how soldiers contrive to fire them at all; and particularly how they keep pace with others that will not bear their own weight when suspended on the trigger. What must be the exertion of the one man to the other, whose trigger draws so easy! I do not allude to air-triggers, but the triggers with common pull, as now used by the ninety-fifth regiment. The gun should neither be over heavy, nor too light; as the extreme of either would prove equally

50 GENERAL OBSERVATIONS.

disadvantageous: in the one case the gun might be made so heavy, that, were the trigger to bear the weight of it, it would cause too great exertion; and, in the other case, if it be made too light, by the same rule it would be very unsafe. The rifles of the ninety-fifth regiment are nine pounds and a half each; and the locks have a fly or scape in the tumbler, to prevent the seer catching at the half-cock, which will frequently happen, if the lock pulls as it ought to do without it; rifles requiring a much lighter pull at the trigger than muskets.

In letting the cock down from full to half-cock, the following directions should be particularly attended to: the thumb of the right hand should be on

GENERAL OBSERVATIONS. 51

the top of the cock over the flint, against
the cock-pin that holds in the flint: hold
it back; with the fore-finger of the right
hand draw the trigger, and let the cock
gradually down towards the pan until it
has passed the half-cock; then draw it
back into the half-cock, which will be
easily ascertained by hearing it click into
the half-bent or catch of the tumbler.
The locks of rifle pieces have in general
a fly or scape in the tumbler of the lock,
which is called a detant, to prevent the
seer catching at the half-cock, which
keeps it from going into the half-cock
until it is let down, and drawn back
as before-mentioned; and consequently
requires particular attention. Indeed the
locks of all fire arms cannot be too carefully noticed, nor the method I have

E 2

52 GENERAL OBSERVATIONS.

suggested be too minutely practised; as I have often found the seer catch on the top of the half-bent of the tumbler instead of going into the bent, which makes it very dangerous; as a shake of the piece, or dropping the butt on the ground, would let it off. Such a mistake has in a great degree induced the report of a gun going off at half-cock; and particularly the lock of soldiers' muskets, which are apt to catch on the half-bent of the tumbler, if not let down and drawn back as before-mentioned. This arises from the half-bent and seer nose being left too wide or too thick, which is frequently the case, but more especially with the locks of muskets. I am not an advocate for the use of air triggers, as they are apt to get out of

GENERAL OBSERVATIONS. 53

repair, and without great care become dangerous. If the locks are made to act as before-mentioned, there will be no occasion for them.

To take a true aim with a cross wind, I recommend the practitioner to make some allowance, as I have ever found that the surest method. Some people fancy the folding elevating sights most eligible: but I confess I have little opinion of their practical utility, as the joints of the sights will work loose from wear, so that there will be little dependance in the truth of them. The sight for the greatest range may be up, when a shot at a shorter distance may offer: in this case the man, not perceiving it, would be much deceived in taking his

GENERAL OBSERVATIONS.

aim; and will require the face to be removed from its stationary place on the stock, to enable the eye to pass over it: thus he will be doubly deceived, as he will have no rest for his cheek. I have found it a more certain way to make allowance in the elevation, rather than to move the face from its stationary place off the stock, to allow the eye to pass over the folding elevating sights, for three hundred yards range. In trying guns I have frequently been deceived by folding elevating sights; for which reason I rely always on one sight, and consider that much more to be depended upon, at all distances. Its shape on the top should represent a sphere of a circle, with a small notch in the centre, so as to admit of the light on each side of

GENERAL OBSERVATIONS. 55

the front sight, which forms itself to the eye better than any sight I have ever yet tried. The back sight should not stand too near the lock; as it will be liable to be filled with filth from the smoke from the pan of the lock, which will be a great denial to taking a true sight through the small notch. The sight cannot be too much simplified, as the object is more easily obtained; and if a man cannot measure his distance with his eye, all the folding, elevating, or telegraphic sights, so wonderfully eulogized, will never realize his expectations; and though perseverance may accomplish much, he may rest assured he will eventually discover his error. One of the principal sciences in shooting is, for a man to measure his distance correctly before he shoots; and,

56 GENERAL OBSERVATIONS.

if he cannot do this, all the sights that can be added will never make him a good shot with rifle, or indeed any other piece. As I have said elsewhere, this may easily be accomplished by adopting the method I have suggested, and by adhering strictly to the rules laid down for judging distances.

Among other new-fangled terms for sights, there is one called the *Diopta*, or telegraph sight; but of which I entertain a poor opinion. However, this I am certain, that whilst the man is taking his aim through this *famous* invention, I could shoot him three times over. From the description of it, I consider it both cumbersome and troublesome, and very liable to be easily dis-

GENERAL OBSERVATIONS. 57

placed. Neither the French, Germans, nor Americans, ever use such a ridiculous *advantage*, as it is called. They use one back sight, which is indeed most certain; and the front sight should be placed as near the nose end of the barrel as possible, and not, as I have occasionally seen them two or three inches off;—this never could have been invented by a *practical* gun maker, or even by a practical rifleman.

A rifleman should first fire from a rest, at a short distance, to ascertain the straight line of his sights; after which he should ascertain the elevation of his rifle at point blank; by which means he will elevate or depress, according to the distance he is from the object he fires at.

58 GENERAL OBSERVATIONS.

The sights on the king's rifles are intended for two hundred yards point blank. A young rifleman should never accustom himself to fire from a rest after he has ascertained the nature of the sights, &c. but should practise the best position to insure steadiness. I have added four different positions, which I consider most easy, and certainly the best calculated for general practice: but I prefer the positions 3 and 4, particularly in windy weather, as most certain, where the object can be obtained. The young rifleman may improve upon these positions, and adopt any other, according to his own judgment, without a fixed rest, as it will frequently happen that he will have no rest when the greatest accuracy is required. Firing at a target fixed

GENERAL OBSERVATIONS.

against a bank of earth, sand, or chalk pit, has given me a much better opportunity of correcting errors, than firing at a small target alone in the middle of an open field. To ascertain the exact elevation or depression of a ball, place a small object either above or below the bull's eye, or centre of the target;—by firing at various distances, the elevation or depression of the ball will be perceptible, and, by taking aim accordingly, you will obtain the greatest accuracy. I suggest these hints to the young practitioner; and strongly recommend him to embrace every opportunity to practise; to make remarks on every variation that occurs; and, by continually noticing the deviation of the ball from its intended object, he will ascertain with precision,

60 GENERAL OBSERVATIONS.

and be enabled to rectify every error that occurs, till at last he becomes a good shot. I have also added two men-targets that I have fired at; with a table of the weight and diameter of lead balls, from one in the pound to one hundred in the pound.

I wish to caution the rifleman never to be in too great a hurry in loading and firing. I have found one shot in a minute as much as I could fire to keep myself steady, and to perform every motion methodically; and let him rest assured, as a general principle, that loading *properly* is much more advantageous than loading *expeditiously*.

When the sun shines strongly in the

GENERAL OBSERVATIONS. 61

face, the brim of the hat is a great protection, as the rays are too powerful for the eyes, unless shaded with something. In ramming down the ball, the air will sometimes force the powder into the touch-hole very hard, which will occasion the rifle to hang fire, or flash in the pan, and not fire the powder in the barrel, particularly in joint or patent breech barrels, as the narrow chamber at the bottom of the patent breech is forced by the powder and the air which the ball drives before it so hard, that the rifle will hang or miss fire more than it will with a plain breech. This I have frequently experienced, and give the preference to plain breeches for rifle barrels. A rifle, when it hangs or misses fire, is a great denial to a rifleman, and, in action, may

62 GENERAL OBSERVATIONS.

be the cause of losing his life. To prevent this, put a picker, made for that purpose, into the touch-hole whilst loading; shut down the hammer on the picker, or the air will blow it out; when loaded, take out the picker, prime, and with the picker force a little powder into the touch-hole. Be careful not to prime too full, as it will prevent the hammer going down, and occasion the prime to be lost, or the damp to get to the priming; which will make the rifle hang or miss fire. A pin or small feather will be equally effective to stop the touch-hole when not provided with a picker.

This mode of loading will do in practice; but in action I am aware many difficulties will arise, and the soldier, from

GENERAL OBSERVATIONS. 63

various causes, may lose the picker. In lieu of a picker or feather, pick the touch-hole after loading; this will loosen the powder, when forced too hard by the loading.

A rifleman should be careful not to have his lock on full cock whilst loading; as, from the pressure of forcing down the ball, it might go off, which might be attended with bad consequences. The bolt that I have invented, under the patronage of His present Majesty, is certainly a preventive against its going to cock, or off at half-cock, until unbolted, as it bolts itself in going to half-cock. This mode of bolting for rifles or pistols will prevent many accidents that have before occurred, and for which I have

64 GENERAL OBSERVATIONS.

received the Silver Medal from the "Society for the Encouragement of Arts, Manufactures," &c. A model of this and several other improvements may be seen at their Repository Room, John Street, Adam Street, Adelphi, in the Strand, and a treatise of which is published in the Transactions of the Society for 1810, (page 201,) wherein several useful hints are given on the subject. It is a peculiar gratification for me to learn, that many of these suggestions have been found useful to the public; more particularly the swivel rammer, high hammer, and backside screw to pistol, musket, and other locks.

To clean a barrel after firing, wash the barrel out with hot or cold

GENERAL OBSERVATIONS. 65

water; after drying the barrel with tow, put a little sweet oil on the tow, or rag, and rub it up and down the barrel. The muzzle of the barrel should always be stopped when not in use, to keep out the air: this will prevent rust, which, every one is aware, must be extremely prejudicial to all rifle barrels and fowling pieces. A rifle barrel should always be kept brown, as it will prevent the glare of the sun obstructing the eye, or dazzling it, which all bright barrels are so apt to do.

There are many ways of introducing the powder into the barrel, by means of charges screwed to the end of the rammer or loading rod, for the purpose of carrying the whole charge of powder to the bottom of the barrel; and which is done

F

GENERAL OBSERVATIONS.

in this manner:—turn the rifle upside down; introduce the charger with the powder, into the nose-end of the barrel; let the rifle gently down the rod, till it touch the bottom; then turn the rifle, and draw out the rod. I explain this method, some gentlemen having expressed their approbation; but, for general use, this will be found troublesome. The following methods answer very well, and I give them a decided preference. Carry a loose measure or charger in the pocket; or fasten it to the button-hole of the coat or jacket by a string, to prevent its being lost:—fill it from the horn or flask, that the charge may be at all times alike, which is not the case with the spring charges; for the cutter that divides the powder in the flask will from constant

GENERAL OBSERVATIONS. 67

wear get loose, and consequently imperceptibly admit more powder into the barrel than the regular charge; or, it will happen not powder enough; as the spring that divides by the thumb sometimes goes back too suddenly, and before the charger is sufficiently filled. This plan may be depended on for all shooting where time and circumstances will permit, as it insures an uniform and equal charge, which I consider indispensable for the true range of the ball: and the ball itself, with its patch, when it fits air-tight, carries all the powder down, and clears the barrel from every particle which may otherwise lodge there.

I have been credibly informed, "that " the balls used by Turks and the

F 2

68 GENERAL OBSERVATIONS.

" Arabs occasion much more terrible
" wounds than those used by Euro-
" pean troops: they have attached to
" each of them a pedicle of iron or cop-
" per, which is united with the lead when
" cast. The iron wire, which is about an
" inch long, enters into the cartridge,
" and sometimes unites two balls to-
" gether. They are besides ragged, and
" of a larger calibre than those of our
" pieces*." I do not pretend to dis-
pute the authority—but I much doubt
the effect. In pieces of ordnance, the
bar or double shot, and the chain-shot,
may, no doubt, do much more execution
than a common ball, but in rifles and

---

* M. Larrey, in his " Memoirs of Military Sur-
geon:" in which he states that many soldiers came under
his direction, wounded with balls of this description.

GENERAL OBSERVATIONS. 69

muskets, I am quite satisfied that no ball can carry true, unless it fits the tube, as I have so frequently enforced.

A rifleman should not blame his rifle if it does not at all times throw the ball to one point. I have seen rifles fixed so as to be immoveable in firing, and yet have varied, as shewn in Appendix, Nos. 1, 2, and 3, and many other experiments that I have attended, in which the same effect has been produced, notwithstanding every care has been taken in loading, &c. The breech-pin in barrel, and false breech and barrel, should be marked on the top with an index, to shew when the breech-pin in barrel is turned to its right mark; by which precaution the sight and touch-hole will

70 GENERAL OBSERVATIONS.

always be kept in the right place. I recommended the Honorable Board of Ordnance to have all muskets marked so, which they thought proper to adopt. By this plan, the soldiers can easily ascertain when the pins are right; and many mistakes are prevented which have before happened; either by their turning the breech-pin in barrel too far, or not far enough, and the touch-hole has consequently been thrown out of its place, either under the pan or over the hammer. When this has occurred, the soldier has been at a loss to account for his musket missing fire, and it has induced a report that guns have been sent out without touch-holes. By the simple method I have recommended, the breech-pins are always in their right place; and the

GENERAL OBSERVATIONS. 71

loops on barrels are kept to their proper stations. The stock has frequently been split when the loops are not placed so as to receive the bolts or wire-pins that hold the barrel in stock. Indeed it is of essential consequence for the soldier, as well as the sportsman, to attend to all these minutiæ, and I am proud to acknowledge the many handsome testimonies I have received of the importance of these suggestions.

It has always been considered that three-fourths, or a whole turn in the angle of rifle in a barrel three feet in length, was the best for throwing a ball to a certainty. This mode of rifling is practised by the Germans, French, and Americans; and all the foreign rifles that

72 GENERAL OBSERVATIONS.

I have ever yet seen are rifled according to that principle; and several English gunmakers are firmly of opinion, that one turn in four feet is the best angle possible. With these angles of rifle I never could fire at a long range to any degree of certainty. If I apportioned the powder to make it range at three hundred yards, I found the ball go very random; and from this I judged that the ball stripped over the top of the rifle, which caused it to fire as random as a common musket. In order to find out the cause of this evil, I rifled a barrel one turn in four feet; and, on trial, found that the nearer I came to the straight line, the more true and further I could range. I then cut it to one foot one quarter turn, and found I could fire more

GENERAL OBSERVATIONS. 73

true at a short distance than I could when more angle in rifle. From this conviction I made a barrel two feet six inches, and rifled in one quarter turn. The experiment succeeded to my most sanguine expectation. I was perfectly satisfied, that I could range further, and more true, than in any previous trial, and with less elevation. In loading also, the friction is not so great, and the ball is not so much impeded in coming out of the barrel by the angle in the rifle more approaching the straight line. Mr. Robins, in his Treatise of Gunnery, page 339, says, " Whatever tends to diminish " the friction in rifle barrel pieces, tends " at the same time to render them more " complete for the service;" but these

74 GENERAL OBSERVATIONS.

experiments I tried before I knew any thing of Mr. Robins's Treatise.

MUCH has been said, and a variety of opinions given by many individuals, respecting the length of gun barrels for throwing small shot and ball with the greatest velocity. I beg leave to observe, that I have made a barrel twenty-three feet in length; have cut it into various lengths, and have joined it together by means of screws, so that it can be fired the whole length, and from the different lengths from joint to joint to three feet in length. I have tried every variation, and found no difference when fired with ball

GENERAL OBSERVATIONS. 75

in its penetrating a board or target; but when fired with small shot, I was astonished at the variation in the same distance, there being a difference of one-third in strength and quantity. Gentlemen, wishing to judge of the best length of barrel for themselves, may be satisfied by trying these experiments at my Manufactory. I have, however, added some SPECIFIC REMARKS on FOWLING PIECES, which will be found worthy the attention of all sportsmen.

AN

EXPERIMENT

TRIED at WOOLWICH, 4th FEBRUARY, 1800,

By Order of the Honorable Board of Ordnance.

In the year 1800, the principal gunmakers in England were directed by the Honorable Board of Ordnance to produce a specimen, in order to procure the best rifle possible, for the use of a rifle corps (the 95th regiment) raised by Government. Among those who were selected on this occasion, I was desired to attend: and a committee of field officers was appointed for the purpose of examining,

SPECIMENS OF RIFLES. 77

and reporting according to their judgment. There were also many rifles from America, and various parts of the Continent produced at the same time. These were all tried at Woolwich: when my barrel, having only one quarter turn, in the rifle, was approved by the committee. It was also remarked, that the barrel was less liable to foul from frequent firing, than the hole three-quarters or half-turns in angles of the rifle, which was considered of great advantage to the corps, particularly when engaged, as they would not require so often sponging out as the greater angles would, and yet possess every advantage of the other rifle in point of accuracy and strength of shooting at three hundred yards distance. For all these reasons the committee gave mine

MY RIFLE PREFERRED.

a preference, and recommended to the Honorable Board of Ordnance to have their rifles made upon a similar construction, the practice of which is shewn in the Appendix, No. 1, fired at a target three hundred yards distance. And in the year 1803, a target was fired at, at two hundred yards distance, by command of his present Majesty, then Prince of Wales, with a rifle barrel twenty inches in length; and, from its accuracy was adopted for the use of the 10th Light Dragoons.

From the information received at various periods from the different officers of the 95th rifle regiment, respecting the rifles made by me for government, in the years 1800 and 1801; it is with infinite

QUARTER-TURN APPROVED. 79

satisfaction I learn, that, although a great variety has been submitted for trial, rifled in different angles, and to load in various ways, by means of screws in the lower end of the barrel; mine have never yet been exceeded in accuracy of shooting, &c. I have also received the thanks of many officers of that corps for the publication of my " Practice;" which, they have been pleased to say, has been most effective in disciplining the corps in firing at the target. And other gentlemen of the first respectability have corroborated their favorable opinion, as well as expressed their approbation of the quarter-turn.

I have made rifles as large as four to the pound; but have found no size to

WEIGHT OF BALLS.

answer so well as that used by the 95th regiment, twenty to the pound. The smaller the ball, the less elevation is required; and I am quite satisfied, that twenty to the pound is more effective than any other. The largest size, on which any dependence can be insured, is fourteen to the pound; but on a larger ball than fourteen, I am assured no reliance whatever can be placed. Besides, there is another, and more important objection to rifles carrying even fourteen to the pound; as they necessarily become too heavy for the soldier in a long day's march. When the 95th regiment was first raised, I made some rifles of equal dimensions to the muskets, in order that they might be supplied, if necessity required, from any infantry regiment that

WEIGHT OF BALLS.　81

might be near them. They were however strongly objected to by the commanding officer, Colonel Manningham, as well as all the officers of the regiment, as requiring too much exertion, and harassing the men from their excessive weight. They were consequently immediately relinquished.

AN

EXPERIMENT

TRIED at WOOLWICH, 15th *MAY*, 1806,

𝕭𝖞 𝕺𝖗𝖉𝖊𝖗 𝖔𝖋 𝖙𝖍𝖊 𝕳𝖔𝖓𝖔𝖗𝖆𝖇𝖑𝖊 𝕭𝖔𝖆𝖗𝖉 𝖔𝖋 𝕺𝖗𝖉𝖓𝖆𝖓𝖈𝖊.

—◄●►—

THE Honorable Board of Ordnance being anxious to ascertain, if rifling a large piece would have the same advantage over smooth barrels, which rifles possess over muskets, and would be equally effective in carrying the ball, the experiment was tried at Woolwich, with two wall-piece barrels of equal dimensions, one rifled, the other not rifled, (the length of the barrels, 4 feet 6 inches; weight,

RIFLED WALL-PIECE BARRELS. 83

20lbs.—weight of the ball, 3 oz. 3 drams, and 5½ grains, or 5 in the lb.): and after each had been fired several times, with various loads of powder, the advantage the rifled wall-piece had was NOT in comparison with the former practice I have had with rifles, with balls twenty to the pound.

PROVING AND RE-PROVING

BARRELS.

I HAVE, at a considerable expense, established a PROOF-HOUSE, under the sanction and patronage of His present Majesty, on my own premises, (the only one in London,) for PROVING and RE-PROVING barrels by Fire, Water, and Target proof, as the only security against those fatal accidents which occur from the bursting of barrels that have only undergone the fire proof, although *that alone* entitles them to the proof-mark established at the Tower and Gun-makers' Proof-houses. In respectfully soliciting the attention of

PROVING BARRELS. 85

the nobility, gentry, and sportsmen in general, to this establishment, I beg to call to their recollection the old adage,— " PREVENTION IS BETTER THAN CURE."

Gentlemen, wishing to have the safety of their gun and pistol barrels ascertained, may see them proved, at any hour of the day, with balls of every size, from one in the pound to one hundred in the pound. The plan pursued by me, for this purpose, is to load the barrel with powder equal to the weight of the ball that fits the bore, of the same strength as is used at the King's Proof-house, according to the rule established from time immemorial, and wisely adopted for public safety; but which has lately been altered by an Act of Parliament obtained

86 PROVING AND

by the Birmingham Proof Company; and also at the Company of Gun-makers' Proof-house in London: by which, however, the proof is reduced to nearly one-third less of powder. As too much care and caution cannot be taken in the proof of gun barrels, and properly examining them after proof, I adopt a second proof, by forcing water in the barrel with a proper apparatus. This will point out the slightest defect, which the eye cannot discern in the first proof; and this second proof will shew the dangerous parts of the barrel, by the oozing out of the water so forced down. From the neglect of proving barrels in this manner, many accidents daily occur, too well known to the public; and the necessity of requiring an additional proof of this

RE-PROVING BARRELS. 87

sort, is evident from specimens of barrels which I have by me, that have been proved as directed by the Act of Parliament, and delivered as safe and fit for use; but, when proved in this manner, I have discovered to be dangerous and totally unfit for use.

The necessity, therefore, of the original proof is apparent to every one—and, although I wish to pay every respect to *improvement*, I consider this rather as an innovation of those principles which were formed for public safety. By the old act, twenty-three drams of powder were required—by the *new*, sixteen drams only are used—consequently, the force is not so great as it would have been, and the defects, if any, are not so easily ex-

PROVING AND

posed. The greater the force of powder, the sooner any imperfection is detected. Great numbers of musket barrels, when cleaned and browned, have been found very defective, although they have been marked and stamped as *sound good* barrels. This has, no doubt, arisen from the *improvement*, as it is called, of lessening the proof; and many accidents have occurred, from the corrosive ingredients used in browning eating into the defective places, which must have been discovered, if a greater force had been used in proving the barrels. In the preamble of this act, " it is requisite, *(for* " *the express purpose of protecting the* " *lives of His Majesty's subjects,)* to les- " sen the quantity of powder in proving " barrels." I think I have proved, that

RE-PROVING BARRELS. 89

the very reverse is more consonant with that feeling—and have therefore only to add on this subject—*from such protection may we have a safe deliverance!*

By the old method, a barrel was obliged to stand three days after proof, before it was examined as to its safety—but proof with water is certainly more efficacious. In the former, the filth from the powder renders any imperfection very difficult to be discovered; and, by standing so long, the barrel becomes corroded by rust: in the latter, the water oozes through the defective parts, and points them out very perceptibly. It was stated in the House of Commons, on the 12th of June, 1816, when a motion was made for a committee to inquire into the manage-

PROVING AND

ment and expenditure of the Small Arms Department under the Board of Ordnance, " that there was an evident mismanage- " ment in the proving of barrels at the " Government factory, which was to be " attributed to the ignorance of the person " superintending that business." The Honorable Member who brought forward the motion, Colonel Palmer, undertook to prove, " that many accidents had oc- " curred from want of due attention to " the proving of barrels, and conse- " quently to the safety of the soldier;" and further added, " that he had lately " seen an officer, who was stationed with " his regiment upon the field of Waterloo, " after the battle, where he had seen a " great quantity of muskets which had " burst in action, and must have de-

RE-PROVING BARRELS. 91

" stroyed the lives and limbs of those who
" had held them."—After an experience
of forty years I can discover no method
so safe as proof by water after powder—
and I have, from that practical knowledge,
adopted it in preference to all other, both
for my own protection, as well as for the
safety of the public; to whom I take
leave strongly to recommend it: and
particularly to gentlemen who have used
their barrels for any length of time, or
whose barrels have been damaged by accident; but more especially to those who are
in the habit of using double barrels that
have not been proved, after being reduced
by filing to join them together. All
guns, rifles, pistols, &c. manufactured by
me, and offered for sale, have undergone
this necessary process; and are warranted

as free from danger as ingenuity, care, and PROOF can make them.

RIFLE guns of very superior quality for shooting tigers are also warranted: and have been highly approved of by gentlemen, as well as by the natives of India.

OF CASTING BALLS.

THERE is much greater attention and nicety required in casting balls than is generally imagined. Care should be taken to avoid both the extremes of heat and cold; as, if the lead be so hot as to boil like water, the ball becomes too light and hard; and if too cold, the lead will not run so as to fill the mould sufficiently, and of course the ball will be too small. An equal temperature is absolutely essential to the casting of balls true. I shall therefore point out the method I consider most eligible, and which is as simple as it is efficacious.

94 OF CASTING BALLS.

When the lead begins to melt in the ladle, put in a little tallow, or any sort of grease, oil, or rosin: stir it up with a piece of thin sheet iron, and the scum and dirt will rise to the top, which of course should be taken off. The molten lead then appears quite clear, and is of a proper temperature for use. If it becomes cold, after taking it off the fire, as it will do, and which is easily ascertained by its hanging together, and by the appearance of a rough grain, it must be melted again: though by repeatedly melting the same lead, it will become hardened similar to pewter.

In making balls, after casting five or six, the mould will frequently become so hot, that the lead will not fit as it ought

OF CASTING BALLS.   95

to do, or the ball will become hollow: in this case, the mould should be put into cold water, closed with a ball so as to prevent the water from getting into it. The mould should then be wiped quite dry. This precaution should be carefully attended to, and the mould moderately warmed over the fire: for, if the hot lead is poured into the mould when wet, it will fly about in every direction, and the face and eyes will be liable to be much burnt. If on the other hand, the mould is too cold, the lead becomes chilled, the ball is rendered too small and too light, and a rough surface spreads over it; to prevent this, I generally melt the first ball over again.

Great care should be taken that

OF CASTING BALLS.

neither pewter, tin, nor plumber's solder be mixed with the lead, particularly in making balls for rifles—as they will be much more difficult to get down the barrel from their hardness; and, besides, they will be thus rendered much lighter, and of course will not range so far nor so true. The lead should be quite pure, to insure good balls, and perfection in shooting with the rifle.

By keeping lead balls close from the air, they acquire a rough powder, very similar to the rust on cast iron, by which they become too large for the guage: if this is removed, it soon forms another, of a dark grey powder. In either case (when removed), the ball is too light; and, consequently, little dependance can

OF CASTING BALLS. 97

be placed on the ball's being of the proper weight or size. And as it is of material consequence to ascertain the precise weight and size, I have made steel guages of one hundred different sizes, rising progressively both in weight and diameter, as may be seen by the tables which are inserted at the end of these " REMARKS."

OF THE BULLET-MOULD.

HAVING described the method of preparing the molten lead for the balls, the next important subject is the MOULD itself: and in those now generally used for casting balls there is an evident imperfection. By the usual method, notwithstanding every care, when the neck or castable is cut off, a small hole is frequently perceptible, which evidently shews that the ball is not perfectly solid; and it also requires considerable nipping and filing off the burrs, to make it perfectly round, which occupies a considerable portion of time. To remedy these imperfections I

OF THE BULLET MOULD. 99

have, at very considerable expense, and with much trouble, invented a NEW MOULD and CLIPPER, which is not only far superior to any yet adopted; but, I trust, will be found as perfect as Art can make it. Previously, however, to submitting it to the test of public approbation, I sent a specimen of my new mould to the *Society for the Encouragement of Arts and Manufactures;* and I am proud to say it has so entirely met their approbation, that

AN HONORARY SILVER MEDAL

has been voted to me for the invention. Although I have annexed a PLATE, with back and front views, describing minutely every part which differs from the old moulds, with an explanation of its various properties, I take leave to insert my

100 OF THE BULLET-MOULD.

letter to the secretary, together with two others—the former, giving a full detail of the improvement—the latter, complimentary to myself, and approving highly of the success which has crowned my exertions. And as balls cannot be cast too true, particularly for rifles, I consider this machine, though simple in its construction, to obviate every difficulty that had previously occurred; and feel assured, when once tried, that every other mould will be instantly discarded.

OF THE BULLET-MOULD. **101**

TO

A. AIKEN, Esq.

Secretary to the Society of Arts, &c.

SIR,

I TAKE leave to request you will lay before the Society a new-invented BULLET-MOULD, which, after considerable expense and infinite labour, I have brought to perfection; and in claiming the merit of the invention, I trust the following explanation of its improvement will be satisfactory to the Society.

Firstly. The mould has a much larger counter-sink on the top, and of course holds a greater quantity of molten

102 OF THE BULLET-MOULD.

lead, which, as it sinks in the mould, prevents that hollowness which is generally found in balls cast from moulds in the former way, and consequently renders them more solid and far superior.

Secondly. The steel-cutter on the top of the mould is, perhaps, the greatest part of the improvement on the old cutter, as will be immediately discovered by cutting off the neck of a ball with each. My invention consists in taking off the castable or neck of the balls, AT ONCE, quite clean, and at the same time to preserve its globular shape: consequently, the labour and time which were formerly devoted in nipping and trimming, or filing off the exuberance from the ball, are by this method entirely saved, and

OF THE BULLET-MOULD. 103

the ball *at one motion* is made perfect. The double advantage of cutting the balls true, and rendering them quite solid, in so short a space of time, must be instantly perceptible to the Society, and is of essential importance to all fire-arms, but more particularly so to rifle-barrels, where the greatest accuracy is required.

Thirdly. Against the cutter is placed a small cup to hold the ball, which renders the cutting off the neck of the ball more easy and expeditious.

Fourthly. Under, and attached to the mould, is placed a solid stud, for the purpose of screwing in a vice when opportunity offers, by which the balls

104 OF THE BULLET-MOULD.

will be cut easier and much faster than by the hand.

Having thus briefly described the new mould, and explained the advantage and superiority of the invention, I have to request you will submit it to the inspection of the Society, as I am most anxious to receive their approval before I offer it to public notice. I shall be happy to furnish any additional information that may be required by the Society, and have the honor to subscribe myself,

Sir,

Your most obedient

And very humble Servant,

EZEKIEL BAKER.

February 8, 1821.
24, WHITECHAPEL ROAD.

The following letters are too flattering to be omitted—and were enclosed to the Secretary of the Society, as evidences of the estimation in which my invention was held by gentlemen, whose experience and judgment are too well known to need any comment.

February 13, 1821.

DEAR SIR,

I FEEL much gratified in the perusal of your description of your new-invented bullet-mould, as to the idea of preventing, as much as possible, the bullets from being less hollow, but particularly your method of cutting off the

106 OF THE BULLET-MOULD.

ends. I have been accustomed to rifle-shooting for six-and-twenty years, and always considered that the accuracy of shooting depended much on the roundness of the ball, which I, in general, filed; but which I conceive is much better accomplished by your circular nipper. I think it deserves the notice particularly of rifle-shooters, and worthy the consideration of the Society of Arts.

I am,

DEAR SIR,

Your very humble Servant,

MICHAEL BRAND.

62, *Jermyn Street,*
ST. JAMES'S.

OF THE BULLET-MOULD. 107

February 13, 1821.

SIR,

I HAVE carefully examined your bullet-mould and nipper, and find it of the greatest utility. As a Hanoverian Yeager, I have always considered that something was wanting to nip off the ends of bullets clean, without the necessity of cutting off the corners afterwards, which is perfectly accomplished by your circular nipper. The advantage, also, of the large orifice in your mould is apparent, as it certainly is much more likely to cast the balls solid. Your improved bullet-mould has therefore my fullest approbation.

I am, SIR,

Your humble Servant,

C. BUCKHOLZ.

Carlton House.

108   OF THE BULLET-MOULD.

After such testimonials, supported by the cordial approbation of the Society of Arts, I have nothing more to add, but this:—that my own experience justifies the recommendation—and that I feel a peculiar gratification in having forged an additional link to the advancement of arts and sciences.

SPECIFIC REMARKS

ON

FOWLING PIECES.

It is not my intention to give an elaborate dissertation on SHOOTING—many works have been printed on that subject, which are more or less interesting, according as circumstances give weight to the argument, or create a smile from the minuteness with which they are detailed. According to Mrs. Glasse —of culinary celebrity—" first catch your fish;" so it is with some of these would-be adepts in the noble exercise of field-

SPECIFIC REMARKS

sports. Some pretend to give "*Direc-tions to young Sportsmen;*" in which they tell you that " old birds are not to be caught with chaff;"—they describe, with peculiar accuracy, the length of the barrel; the elevation and sight; the stock, breeching, and touch-hole; the locks, springs, and hammer; with various other particulars, " too numerous to be eluci-" dated in the small compass of a few " sheets of instructions for excelling in " shooting." They wisely tell you " to keep your gun moving:" that before an object, you must level your piece *cross-ing;* and *full high,* for a bird rising; that you must consider the velocity with which a bird flies, and the fleetness of hares and rabbits—that for the former, you must fire at least six inches before

ON FOWLING PIECES. 111

it; and for the latter, between the ears: and, in the same breath, gravely recommend you to fix your eye on the object, and fire the moment you have brought up your gun. Others again attempt to point out the best method of " Shooting flying;" with directions for the choice of guns; and various experiments to discover the execution of barrels of different lengths and bores; with useful hints, &c.

Now, these may be all very well in their way—and doubtless have met with the encouragement they deserve. I could very easily give a variety of anecdotes which might afford much amusement to my readers, — and which, though supported by *unquestionable* authority, certainly appear " wondrous marvellous."

112　　SPECIFIC REMARKS

I could expatiate on the perils of the "tented field"—and tell of "battles fought and battles won"—and could travel over the "Field of Waterloo"— pointing out

" Those hostile fields, where unrelenting Mars
" Sweeps through the falling ranks his scythed cars;
" Lopped from the trunk, the warrior's members fly,
" Purple the ground, and quiver as they lie:
" Where glory's energies the soul engage,
" Flushed with triumphant hope, and fired with rage;
" Where the maimed body urge upon the foe,
" Inspire with courage, and impel the blow—
" Dismembered heroes press the town's assault,
" Scale the high walls, or o'er the ramparts vault;
" Nor miss the severed limb, or battered shield,
" They left behind them on the gory field:
" Where flame the threat'ning eyes with living ire,
" Nor close, till flown the soul's indignant fire."

But as my object is rather to give a

FOWLING PIECES. 113

brief view of FOWLING-PIECES, I shall leave the *practical test* to the game-keeper, or to those who take pleasure in

"Teaching the young idea how to SHOOT."

In a preceding part of these "RE-MARKS," I have stated, that, by way of experiment, I had tried various lengths of barrels, with joints to be removed at pleasure; which have served rather for amusement than use: but, after an experience, which will justify an opinion founded on practice, I am assured the following will answer every purpose for field-sports, and will do as much execution as may reasonably be required.

SINGLE BARREL.—2 feet, 10 inches, and 13 balls to the pound; weight, 3 lbs.

114 SPECIFIC REMARKS ON

4 oz.—for its load, $2\frac{1}{4}$ drams of powder, and $2\frac{1}{4}$ oz. of shot.

Ditto.—2 feet 10 inches, and 17 balls to the pound; weight 3 lbs.—for its load, 2 drams of powder, and 2 oz. of shot.

Ditto.—2 feet 8 inches, and 13 balls to the pound; weight, 3 lbs.—of powder, 2 drams, and of shot, 2 oz.

Ditto.—2 feet 8 inches, and 17 balls to the pound; weight, 2 lbs. 12 oz.—of powder, 2 drams, and of shot, 2 oz.

The average weight of a single-barrelled gun should be from 6 lbs. to 6 lbs. 4 oz.

FOWLING PIECES. 115

For wood or cover.—2 feet 6 inches, or 2 feet 4 inches, of the preceding dimensions, I consider the best adapted for this amusement.

———◄●►——

DOUBLE BARRELS.—2 feet 8 inches, and 18 balls to the pound; weight 3 lbs. 10 oz.—of powder, $1\frac{1}{4}$ dram, and of shot, $1\frac{3}{4}$ oz.

Ditto.—2 feet 6 inches, and 18 balls to the pound; weight, 3 lbs. 6 oz.—of powder, $1\frac{3}{4}$ dram, and of shot, $1\frac{3}{4}$ oz.

Weight of gun, 6 lbs. 12 oz.

Ditto.—2 feet 8 inches, and 22 balls to the pound; weight, 3 lbs. 9 oz.—of powder, $1\frac{1}{2}$ dram, and of shot, $1\frac{1}{3}$ oz.

116 SPECIFIC REMARKS ON

Ditto.—2 feet 6 inches, and 22 balls to the pound; weight, 3 lbs. 5 oz.—of powder, 1½ dram, and of shot 1½ oz.

Weight of gun, from 6 lbs. 4 oz. to 6lbs. 8 oz.

Frequent accidents occur with double-barrelled guns—and as I am anxious to put every one on his guard, I will endeavor to point out in what manner they happen, and how to prevent them. It is a common occurrence, that gentlemen usually fire the right-hand barrel at a single bird; and if another do not rise to discharge his left-hand barrel, he will continue to fire the same barrel for many hours. In this case, the charge in the other barrel will become loose :—and

FOWLING PIECES. 117

the same will occur with the right, if the
left be fired first. When the shot by this
practice becomes loose, the air will find
its way between the powder and shot,
and there is then great danger of the
barrel bursting. To prevent such a ca-
tastrophe, when you charge the barrel
which has been fired, put your ramrod
down the other, or loaded barrel; by
which means, both charges become solid,
and no danger can accrue. By this method, however, I have known much trouble arise by carelessness. For example:
having reloaded with powder the barrel
fired off — many gentlemen, who are
aware of the necessity of ramming down
the charge in the other barrel, leave the
rammer in the one while they put the
shot into the other — and it sometimes

118   SPECIFIC REMARKS ON

happens, from hurry or some other cause, that a few shots will fall into that barrel where the ramrod remains quiet, and thus fix it so tight that it is not easy to remove it. In this case, the piece must be turned upside down, and the ramrod gently moved; when the shot, so fallen in, will come out. Of course the charge of shot in the other barrel will fall out too, as there is no wadding to prevent it. I mention this last trifling loss of shot, as even that may be saved by turning the gun over into your hand.—I have also known barrels burst from the sportsman falling, or from getting dirt or snow in the muzzle,—in either of which cases, the gun should never be fired until it has been carefully inspected for the former, and perfectly cleaned from the latter.

FOWLING PIECES. 119

Duck, or Wild Fowl.—3 feet 8 inches, and 10 balls; weight, 6 lbs. 4 oz. — of powder, $3\frac{1}{2}$ drams, and of shot, $3\frac{1}{2}$ oz.

Ditto.—3 feet 4 inches, and 12 balls; weight, 5 lbs. 8 oz.—of powder, 3 drams, and of shot, 3 oz.

Weight of gun, from 8 lbs. to $10\frac{1}{2}$ lbs.

I consider, that all fowling pieces exceeding the above in weight would be attended with no possible advantage, but would be rather cumbersome to the sportsman in general.

120 SPECIFIC REMARKS ON

I do not wish to lay down the preceding as rules from which no deviation should be made under particular circumstances — I have detailed them rather as a guide for YOUNGER SPORTSMEN. The EXPERIENCED will be aware, that nothing but practice will give the average proportion of powder and shot to each fowling piece; as it is well known, a specific charge apportioned to one gun will not do for another; as, indeed, will be seen by referring to my " Table of the Weights and Dimensions of Balls and Small Shot:" but, from my own experience, I am warranted in recommending the above as the best criterion on which to form a judgment.

Respecting the PATENT BREECH, as

FOWLING PIECES. 121

it is called, for firing the powder from
the centre of the barrel, I am of opinion
none is superior to the one for which the
late Mr. Henry Nock obtained a patent.
I was at that period in the employ of
Mr. Nock, and we were both aware that
much improvement might be made in
firing the powder. By the old method,
the powder, when fired, strayed different
ways in communicating from the pan to
the charge—in this, it gave a greater
quickness in firing, and had the decided
advantage of throwing the shot with
additional strength. It was considered
so far superior, that various imitations
were immediately set on foot—but Mr.
Nock's invention has never been sur-
passed. The period allotted for the patent
has some time expired—and it has now

122 SPECIFIC REMARKS.

become general all over the kingdom, and has been adopted in various foreign countries.

There is no regular rule that can apply to the STOCKING OF GUNS, as some gentlemen require a longer or more crooked stock than others—and, consequently, what suits one will not do for another. In sending to any gunmaker, the exact dimensions should be taken, either from an old fowling piece to which the sportsman has been accustomed, or from a regular measure made for that purpose.

BURSTING OF BLUNDERBUSSES.

THOUGH this division does not *actually* come under the description of FOWLING PIECES, it is too important to be omitted in a work, professedly written for the benefit of those who are in the habit of using fire-arms, whether from necessity or for pleasure. And though noticed *last*, is not the *least* important for the consideration of those to whom I have more particularly addressed these RE-MARKS: and especially, as, perhaps, a greater number of accidents arise from the bursting of BLUNDERBUSSES, than from any other description of fire-arms.

124 BLUNDERBUSSES.

The newspapers, indeed, teem with melancholy details of accidents frequently occurring — where, if the party escape with the loss of a finger, an arm, or an eye, he considers himself more fortunate than those whose lives have been sacrificed by the bursting of the barrel. BRASS blunderbusses are certainly most dangerous: as they are too frequently made from bad materials, in order to enable the vendor to dispose of them at a low price. Exclusively of which, they are generally neglected; and are laid by for months, and sometimes years; when they are suddenly produced, and considered *safe* from not having been used for so long a period—and *this very cause*, perhaps, renders them more dangerous; particularly if they have remained loaded

BLUNDERBUSSES. 125

during the time, as the rust eats into the barrel. This last remark applies to barrels of all descriptions; but more especially to those of brass, as they cannot possess the same texture as iron, nor stand the same proof. More accidents happen to the person firing, than to the thief at whom it may be fired; and, consequently, what they think a *protection*, becomes their misery. I therefore, press this observation on ALL—that blunderbusses should be made of the best materials; should be proved, as other firearms; should be frequently examined, and re-proved. Perhaps—and here I do not mean to cast the slightest reflection on those respectable pawnbrokers who dispose of fire-arms second-hand — it would be the safest method, and certainly

126 BLUNDERBUSSES.

the most prudential, for purchasers of fire-arms in general to apply to established makers, whose credit and respectability depend on selling genuine articles; and whose practical experience prevents the possibility of deception, either as to the quality or safety of the barrel.

CONCLUSION. 127

IN CONCLUSION—I have to press on the attention of every sportsman, the absolute necessity of having his fowling piece repeatedly examined, which will prevent those numerous accidents which are so often noticed in the public papers, and which involve, perhaps, a whole family in despair.

Once a year at least it should be sent to the gunmaker, to be minutely inspected, and re-proved if required; and in no instance should he attempt to fire it after a fall, or any other mischance, to which all are liable, before it has undergone the necessary inspection.

128 CONCLUSION.

I now take my leave, in the hope, that my humble endeavors will be duly appreciated—that the hints I have thrown out may be serviceable to all—and to repeat, and to impress upon the memory the important and invaluable adage, that

PREVENTION IS BETTER THAN CURE.

EZEKIEL BAKER.

June, 1821.

SUPPLEMENT

TO

THE EIGHTH EDITION.

June, 1822.

HAVING in the preceding pages entered so fully into the general subject of fire arms, with all the advantages to be derived from the improvements I have suggested in the result of " forty years practice and observations on rifle guns and fowling pieces in general," it would, perhaps, be deemed presumption to extend those observations—but having received a THIRD SILVER MEDAL for an additional improvement in fire arms, I take leave, first, to lay before my Patrons, my letter to the Society of Arts, &c. explanatory of a *further invention*; and

* K

130 SUPPLEMENT.

shall, secondly, draw some conclusions on the benefits to be derived from its introduction; which may tend, eventually, to " PERFECT THE SYSTEM" for the benefit of my Country, in case any future war may call into action the result of additional experience, continued labour, and extraordinary expense.

LETTER TO THE SOCIETY.

TO

A. AIKEN, Esq.

Secretary to the Society of Arts, Commerce, Manufactures, &c.

SIR,

In taking leave to request you will lay before the Society the accompanying model of an improvement in GUN-LOCKS, I trust the merit of the invention will induce the Society duly to appreciate its advantages; and shall consider the labour and expense as amply

132 LETTER TO THE SOCIETY.

compensated by their approbation. The following explanation is necessary to the clearly comprehending the advantages to be derived from its adoption.

It is well known that the main-springs of locks to every description of fire arms lose their strength, either from wear, or from climate; as also that the flints become thick from wear; either of which is of itself sufficient to cause the lock to miss fire. This was, perhaps, more particularly exemplified by the Volunteer Regiments, on field days, when embodied during the late war; and the fact has been corroborated by many veteran soldiers as having occurred too frequently on the field of battle. What can be so distressing to a brave fellow as filling up the ranks merely to be fired at, and feeling at the same time conscious of his own inability to do his duty? He is, from either of these

REGULATING SCREW PIN. 133

causes, disabled from returning the fire, and remains like an automaton, venting condemnation against his musket, or, rather, against the maker.

Now, Sir, my invention will remove all this; and may be easily effected by the soldier with the common turnscrew, which it is well known he invariably carries to put in his flint, &c. It consists of a REGULATING SCREW PIN, which is placed behind the hammer, through the solid piece of the plate. This pin, when screwed down, acts upon the short side of the mainspring; by forcing which its strength is increased, and more fire is consequently drawn from the hammer; so that, in either of the instances alluded to, fire is produced when it would otherwise fail; and, on the other hand, when a new flint is introduced, the power of the mainspring may be lessened, by turning the screw-pin backwards: by

134 LETTER TO THE SOCIETY.

which means the flint is prevented from breaking, as frequently happens when it is put into locks upon their present construction. Having alluded to the more important consideration of rendering musket locks perfect on the field of battle, the same will apply to gentlemen sportsmen, and will prevent the vexation and disappointment that too frequently occur from locks missing fire, when an experienced shot would otherwise make sure of bagging his game. I have for many months felt all its advantages; and have the satisfaction of testimonials from some of the most experienced gamekeepers, whose whole lives have been devoted to the sports of the field: those of His Grace the Duke of Bedford, Lord Petre, and Sir Thomas Lennard, would of themselves be sufficient; but I have others from private individuals equally flattering to my improvements, and to the simplicity of the invention.

REGULATING SCREW. 135

I should remark, that, to all new locks this invention can be applied without any additional expense; but to old locks, in most instances, it will be necessary to have a new mainspring; as the stud, which holds it steady on the plate, is usually placed on the middle of the short side of the spring, and, consequently, the REGULATING SCREW applied to this may chance to break itself, or break the mainspring; whereas in a new lock I place the stud on the bend of the spring, which enables it to play at pleasure without fear of injuring the one or the other. I also make the hole in the eye of the spring oblong, so as to enable it to play more easily up or down, as occasion may require, than the round hole admits.

This invention may be applied with equal effect to the locks of doors and spring bolts of every description, when

136 ADVANTAGE OF THE IMPROVEMENT.

from weakness or any other cause the springs lose their power; and the great advantage is, that my improvement may be adopted at a very trifling expense. Having explained the simplicity with which my invention may be applied, I will not take up more of your valuable time, but shall be happy to wait on the Society at their convenience, and furnish every information which may be required for a clearer elucidation than I may be able to convey on paper.

I have the honor to be,

SIR,

Your obedient Servant,

EZEKIEL BAKER.

24, WHITECHAPEL ROAD,
February 17, 1822.

MEETING OF THE SOCIETY. 137

On Wednesday, the 29th of May, 1822, the SOCIETY OF ARTS held their Annual Meeting for the distribution of premiums, at the Theatre Royal, Drury Lane:

HIS ROYAL HIGHNESS THE

DUKE OF SUSSEX IN THE CHAIR.

The object of this Society is so well known and so truly appreciated, that it would be presumption in me to draw public attention to the benefits derived from a combination of rank and talent in the distribution of rewards for inventions, perhaps unprecedented in the annals of Science—but when we see industry rewarded, manufactures encouraged, and every attention paid to talent, however humble, if it may tend to public advantage, surely it is not the least eulogium to ROYALTY that it condescends to patronize every thing that may add to

138 DISTRIBUTION OF PREMIUMS.

increase the stores of our happy country
—and thus, by encouraging " Arts, Commerce, and Manufactures," endeavoring
to raise Old England to an eminence in the
estimation of foreigners, for the arts of
PEACE, as she has been " placed in the
battle's front" for the protection of all we
hold dear,—our Laws, our Liberty, and
our Religion.

There were no less than one hundred
and eighteen premiums awarded for improvements—In AGRICULTURE AND RURAL
ECONOMY--POLITE ARTS--MANUFACTURES
—CHEMISTRY AND MINERALOGY—MECHANICS—and in COLONIES AND TRADE.

In MECHANICS, No. 12, I had the
honor of receiving the *Silver Vulcan
Medal*, for " an improved mainspring in
fire-arms"—and it might be deemed as a
species of vanity, were I to enumerate the

INVALUABLE BENEFIT. 139

eulogiums I received for the simplicity of my invention. Its benefits are indeed invaluable, either as appertaining to " war's destructive power," or for the more general temperature of an Englishman's soul —field sports and rational recreation.— The reward of the Society is sufficient to stamp its merit—but I aspire to a greater satisfaction—that of serving my country, when necessity may require the " utmost means" for her protection in war—or conduce to the recreation and amusement of her sons in the " piping time of peace."

ON GUNS RECOILING,

AND

THE STOCKING OF GUNS.

January, 1823.

IN pages **30, 31,** I have stated that "Complaint is often made of guns recoiling. Every one that is in the habit of shooting endeavors to put the butt in the hollow of his shoulder, to bring it as near to the centre of his body as possible, in order to prevent shooting across, which is often imperceptibly done, and which excites the wonder of the practitioner that he is so far from striking the object he aims at: this has frequently occurred to me, particularly when in a hurry to fire."

The same complaint has been made by many sportsmen; and as a remedy

A NEW MACHINE. 141

for the defect, I have adopted an expedient as simple as it is efficacious. There is certainly no regular rule, as I have remarked in page 122, for the stocking of guns—some gentlemen requiring a longer or more crooked stock than others; and, consequently, what will suit one will not do for another. For the purpose, therefore, of arranging every gun to the individual sight, and at the same time to prevent the recoiling of the piece, I have invented a machine, which may be called, simply, a MEASURE; and which will not only be a source of amusement to the amateur sportsman, but will tend eventually to perfection in the art of gunnery. To explain myself however more fully. I would recommend a young rifleman and sportsman to present his piece before a looking glass, the same as if in the act of firing at an object—and to take especial notice if his eye is straight along the barrel

142 A NEW MACHINE.

to the point intended, or whether it diverges to the right or left; and, when straight upon the object, on what part of the shoulder he fixes the butt end. This will give him a general view of correctness: for it is not always the fault of not holding the gun straight that causes him to miss his mark—as this frequently arises from the stock being crooked in the butt, or, as it is technically called, cast off either to the right or the left, when neither is required; and from which a wrong sight is taken at the object across the barrel. This will easily be perceived by the method I propose of standing before a glass: as, when the piece is thus presented, stocked straight, and the butt placed in the right part of the shoulder, so that the breech of the barrel and sight form a straight line to the eye, the greatest precision is attained. These are essential points to be attended to, particu-

FOR TAKING TRUE SIGHT. 143

larly in shooting flying. Some gentlemen kill a right hand shot with great certainty, while others kill a left hand shot with equal precision. The stocking of a gun in a right line to suit different individuals is an essential requisite, but which is too often neglected; though, if strictly adhered to, it is of more importance than is commonly conceived: for if a barrel or the *material* be ever so good, and is not placed right in the stock, it is a great chance if the piece shoots to any degree of certainty. By my machine, or MEASURE, every gentleman may convince himself of its correctness by repeating the experiment before a looking glass, and arranging the sight to his own convenience. In fact, every person can be accommodated as to sight—by a long or short stock, or a long or short barrel, by elevating or depressing the barrel—and, without entering minutely into all the advantages to be

144 PERFECTION ATTAINED.

derived from an adoption of the principle, I can confidently appeal to many respectable gentlemen who have tried the experiment, and who have been satisfied that, TILL NOW, they were ignorant of the general principle of SHOOTING FLYING—but which, by this simple process, is rendered of easy accomplishment. An application to my Factory will fully satisfy the most fastidious; and convince every one, not only of the ease by which they may suit themselves, but at the same time prove the unerring principle on which the machine is conducted—forming at once a SURE GUIDE, and conducing to perfection in the use of fowling pieces and rifles.

ON PERCUSSION LOCKS.

In page 113, I have stated that I have tried various lengths and weight of barrel, with joints to be removed at pleasure; and the conclusion I then drew has been corroborated by the testimony of the most experienced Sportsmen. In page 118, I endeavored to point out the frequent accidents that occurred from double-barrelled guns, with a remedy to prevent them. Unfortunately, however, the newspapers, on authority too seriously corroborated by publishing the names of the parties to be doubted, daily add to the melancholy list,

146 ADVANTAGES.

—and my attention has been consequently drawn to the subject with renewed anxiety to discover the causes, in the hope of averting so dreadful a calamity. But whether these accidents arise more from the percussion than the common flint lock, it would, perhaps, be indecorous in me to decide, whatever opinion I may individually entertain of their advantages or disadvantages. I will, however, give my views of the former as regards the percussion lock, and at the same time point out what I conceive to be its defects.

ADVANTAGE.—By the detonating or percussion principle, the whole of the powder is fired instantaneously; but the very quickness with which the powder is

DISADVANTAGES. 147

burnt, in my opinion, lessens its general effect; and I am satisfied more execution will be done at equal distance with the charge from the common flint. Indeed, I have proved this fact, by many experiments from the same barrel. In rain, or snow, the percussion lock will act, from its detonating power, more correctly than the common flint lock; and this, by Sportsmen, is considered its greatest, and, I must confess it appears to me its only, advantage.

DISADVANTAGES.—Although the powder in the barrel is fired much quicker, the barrel is necessarily more strained; and to this cause I attribute most of the accidents arising from the bursting of bar-

148 DISADVANTAGES.

rels: as it stands to reason that the suddenness of the ignition requires a greater thickness at the breech, and consequently that the barrel must either bulge or break, if it be not of sufficient thickness to resist the power of the charge. This observation applies more particularly to double-barrelled guns when fired by percussion: and in all descriptions the recoil to the shoulder is more powerful. If, on the other hand, I reduce the quantity of powder to prevent the chance of bursting, or to lessen the force of the recoil; then I can decide, from repeated experiments, that the same charge from the common flint lock is more effective, and throws the shot with more strength and in greater quantity to the object; and I am corro-

ON LOADING. 149

borated in this result by the practical test of many scientific Sportsmen. I may be allowed to add, that, in my judgment, the percussion locks *may mend a bad fowling piece ;* but I never found it of peculiar advantage to a good one.

In LOADING, likewise, I give the preference to the common flint locks which are suffered to prime themselves, and which all will do more or less. In the percussion lock, the detonating pellet for priming is to be placed in its proper receptacle, and consequently a portion of time is occupied. The pellet or copper cap for the percussion also, causes more rust in the lock than powder; and it is not only most difficult to clean, but equally so to keep clean:

150 IMPORTANT HINTS.

besides, it being of a corrosive nature, it will eat away much sooner than the common powder, and which in time will be found very dangerous.

In the common lock, it is usual to prime before charging the gun: the consequence of which is—that the pan is frequently overfilled, and before an opportunity may occur to fire off the piece, the powder is pressed so hard by the hammer in the pan, that when struck off, it hangs fire, and in some instances will not fire at all. This applies more particularly to fire-arms kept loaded for protection. But whether for this purpose, or for the field, equal disappointment arises: in the one case, the Sportsman is balked of his game, and, in

IMPORTANT HINTS. 151

the other, the thief escapes from the punishment he so richly deserves. In both, it is necessary frequently to examine the pan, and when found to be pressed too hard, the prime must be loosened or taken out, and the touch-hole cleaned with a pin or pricker. An experienced Sportsman will, indeed, seldom put too much prime in the pan; and, after charging, will examine it; and if the powder be too hard pressed, will loosen it, or throw it away, and prime afresh—but, though this will prevent the inconveniences I have mentioned, yet it takes up much time, which is entirely obviated by the locks that prime themselves, when hollowed in the hammer-seats — a plan, now generally adopted—and which consequently allows

152 IMPORTANT HINTS.

sufficient space for the prime to enter the pan. The same general remark applies to the rifle, as well as to every fowling piece.

By this means, the powder lies loose in the pan, and consequently fires quicker —the time of priming is saved, and the hammer seat does not get clogged by the powder hanging or sticking to it—as is frequently the case, particularly in hazy weather, when the prime will adhere to the hammer-seat in one solid cake, and is carried up with it. A little caution, however, is even here necessary. The hammer should be shut down on the pan before you begin to load, as I have stated in a former part of these " REMARKS;"

PROOF MOST IMPORTANT. 153

or the powder will be forced through the touch-hole : and a small portion of powder above the usual charge should also be added to allow for priming. I would likewise recommend waddings of hat, pasteboard, or card, in preference to paper, as the air will escape in inserting the latter, and by this means, perhaps, a sufficient quantity of priming may not be forced into the pan: whereas by either of the waddings just named, the piece is certain to be properly primed.

If, however, Gentlemen, therefore, *for its advantages*, prefer the percussion to the common flint lock, I would strongly recommend to them the following important consideration:—To be very cautious in the choice of fowling pieces; to PROVE

154 ACCIDENTS PREVENTED.

the barrel by the percussion principle, particularly in double-barrels: as, in both, the suddenness of the ignition being confined in a narrow compass, naturally strains the barrel, and causes it to burst— thus ascertaining if the breech be made of sufficient strength of metal to meet its power: and I cannot too often repeat the caution, to submit every fowling piece to the PROOF and inspection of competent judges.

This, and this alone, I am satisfied will prevent many of the accidents which so frequently occur from the bursting of barrels by the percussion, and indeed every other lock; and although, as I have before remarked, it is impossible to ascertain

CAUTION. 155

precisely whether the greater number, either of loss of eyes, of fingers, or hands, or even death itself, arise from the one description of lock or the other; yet the hope of benefiting my fellow-countrymen has induced me to submit my opinion to their consideration, by earnestly calling their attention to a subject of such essential importance: and I shall feel the highest gratification, if, by these observations, I should be the humble means of lessening so much of human misery.

One other observation I must be allowed to make—and that is, to caution every person from presenting fire-arms towards another, whether in joke, or for the avowed purpose of frightening them.

156 CONCLUSION.

Many fatal accidents have arisen from this cause; and families have been involved in the extreme of wretchedness, by the casual discharge of a piece which has frequently been attempted to have been fired in vain; and which, from repeated trials, has consequently been supposed not to have been loaded.

Having pointed out, not only the causes of accidents, but their remedies, and thus enabled every man to avoid them, I shall now, conclude my " REMARKS," by enforcing the old, often repeated, and never-to-be forgotten adage, which should be the motto of every Sportsman—that

PREVENTION IS BETTER THAN CURE.

THE END.

INDEX,

OR

ANALYSIS OF THE WORK.

DEDICATION, by Permission, to the KING.

Page

INTRODUCTION 1

Acknowledgment for exalted Patronage.

Theory and practice combined.

Subject arranged under specific divisions.

OF LOADING...................... 5

Portion of powder for rifles, and method
of placing the ball, with directions for
its true flight.

K

130 INDEX.

OF LOADING—*continued.*

Necessity of keeping the grooves of rifles air-tight.

Steel rammers for hammering in the ball objected to, as tending to bruise and injure the barrel.

Importance of marking the rammer at the muzzle end of the barrel.

Method of loosening the ramrod, when fixed in the barrel, by the wadding getting round the tip of the rammer —*now first described.*

Drawing the ball when the powder may have been blown out at the touch-hole—a remedy as simple as it is efficacious, and highly approved of by general officers.

Causes of guns frequently missing fire, and imperfection of the flint explained, with a remedy to prevent it.

INDEX. 131

OF PRESENTING AND TAKING AIM... 28

General directions.

Best position.

The object sooner attained by opening both
eyes, explained.

Advice to young sportsmen — by which
they will obtain confidence.

OF JUDGING DISTANCES............ 38

Hints given as to the best method of at-
taining this object.

The flight of the ball materially affected
by the wind, by rain, and by snow—
and by firing over water or swamps—
with directions for practice.

Greatest range for sure firing.

132 INDEX.

GENERAL OBSERVATIONS............ 42

Preceding remarks casually referred to.

Importance of fixing the sword or bayonet on fire-arms, elucidated.

Improvement in the sight.

Experiment to ascertain whether the rifle carries to the right or left, with directions for remedying any defect.

Plan for ascertaining whether the lock is too strong or too weak for the rifle or musket.

Important direction in letting the cock down from full to half-cock, by which precaution the chance of an accident is prevented.

Reports of guns going off at half-cock, fallacious.

Measuring distance correctly, one of the principal sciences in shooting.

The *Diopta*, or Telegraph Sight, never used by French, Germans, or Americans—and certainly not invented by a PRACTICAL gun-maker.

INDEX. 133

GENERAL OBSERVATIONS—*continued.*

Method to ascertain the exact elevation or depression of a ball.

Loading *properly* more advantageous than loading *expeditiously.*

Cause of guns hanging fire, or flashing in the pan.

Bolts for rifles and pistols, to prevent accidents—for which a SILVER MEDAL was awarded by the " Society for the Encouragement of Arts and Manufactures."

Precautions in cleaning barrels.

Balls used by the Arabs and Turks, singular effect of, and great destruction occasioned by.

Importance of keeping the breech-pins in their right place.

Whatever tends to diminish the friction in rifle barrel pieces, renders them more complete for service.

Variation in guns of different lengths.

134 INDEX.

An EXPERIMENT, tried at Woolwich, February
4, 1800, by order of the Honorable
Board of Ordnance.............. 76

Specimens of rifles.

Baker's rifle preferred, by a committee of
officers appointed by the Board.

Quarter-turn approved by gentlemen of the
highest consideration.

Weight of balls—greatest reliance to be
placed on balls fourteen to the pound.

An EXPERIMENT, tried at Woolwich, May 15,
1806, by order of the Honorable Board
of Ordnance.................. 82

Rifle wall-piece barrels, not possessing the
same advantage as rifles.

INDEX. 135

OF PROVING AND RE-PROVING BAR-
RELS...................... 84

Proof-house, the ONLY ONE in London,
established at 24, Whitechapel Road.

Proof described.

Method formerly adopted at the Government Proof-house objected to.

Reasons for this objection.

Comparisons of proof by the old Act and
that adopted by the *New*—the former,
really for the protection of His Majesty's subjects—the latter, *professing*
to have that object in view, but decidedly the reverse.

PREVENTION BETTER THAN CURE.

Proof by water, the best means of ascertaining the safety of rifles, fowling
pieces, &c.

SUPERIOR RIFLES for tiger shooting.

136 INDEX.

OF CASTING BALLS................ 91

A medium heat requisite, and great attention required.

Steel guages necessary, for ascertaining the precise weight and size of balls.

Pure lead of essential consequence in casting balls—neither pewter, tin, nor plumber's solder admissible.

OF THE BULLET MOULD............. 95

Imperfection of the mould in general use.

Superiority of a New Mould and Clipper, invented by me; and for which the " Society of Arts," &c. have voted me a Second Honorary Silver Medal.

Letter to the Society, giving a minute description of the invention, and pointing out its general advantages.

INDEX. 137

OF THE BULLET MOULD—*continued.*

Letters sent to the Society, highly recommending the new Mould and Clipper:

From M. BRAND, Esq. Jermyn Street.

From C. BUCKHOLZ, Esq. Carlton House
Palace.

SPECIFIC REMARKS ON FOWLING
PIECES 106

Anecdotes not necessary to explain the true
principles of gunnery.

" To teach the young idea how to SHOOT,"
left to the gamekeeper, &c.

SINGLE BARREL — its length, weight, and
charge.

Various sizes.

Those best adapted for field sports.

For wood and cover.

DOUBLE BARREL — its length, weight, and
charge.

L

SPECIFIC REMARKS ON FOWLING PIECES—*continued.*

Accidents, arising from firing *one* barrel for hours; and, *vice versa.*

Directions for preventing them.

Carelessness exemplified.

Barrels bursting from sportsmen falling, or from dirt or snow getting into the barrel.

Duck, or Wild Fowl Gun — its length, weight, and charge.

No advantage derived from fowling pieces of greater power.

Rules laid down meant as a guide to younger sportsmen.

Average proportion of powder and shot to each fowling piece, best ascertained by experience.

INDEX. 139

SPECIFIC REMARKS ON FOWLING PIECES—*continued.*

Patent-breech, invented by Henry Nock, the greatest improvement—its advantages; and general use.

Stocking of guns—no established principle applicable in all cases.

Dimensions of, how taken.

OF BURSTING OF BLUNDERBUSSES. 123

Importance of this division—*last*, though not *least.*

More liable to accidents than other fire-arms.

Brass blunderbusses most dangerous—and why.

Blunderbusses kept loaded, and suddenly produced as *safe* from not having been used, carefully to be guarded against.

140 INDEX.

OF BURSTING OF BLUNDERBUSSES—

continued.

Expected *protection* sometimes produces
the greatest misery.

Second-hand fire-arms—advice respecting.

CONCLUSION   127

Necessity of examination.

Old adage repeated—PREVENTION BETTER
THAN CURE.

SUPPLEMENT.   129

Additional improvement in gun-locks, of a
REGULATING SCREW PIN—submitted to
the " Society of Arts," for which a
THIRD SILVER MEDAL was awarded.

Testimony of experienced gamekeepers.

The invention applied to locks of doors and
spring bolts of every description.

Premiums awarded by the Society.

INDEX. 141

ON GUNS RECOILING, and STOCKING

OF GUNS. . . . ., ... 140

New machine, by which gentlemen may
prove, or take measure of their fowling-
pieces, so as to take true sight, and,
eventually, to attain perfection in the
art of shooting flying.

ON PERCUSSION LOCKS. 145

Their advantage.

Their disadvantages.

Common flint-lock more effective.

Of loading—the common flint lock preferable.

Important information on priming; and the
decided advantage of locks which
prime themselves when hollowed in
the hammer-seats, over the percussion
locks.

Wadding.

142 INDEX.

Hints to gentlemen preferring the percussion locks.

Caution from presenting fire-arms, whether in joke, or for the avowed purpose of frightening another.

Accidents frequently arising from this cause.

Necessary PROOF and inspection, to prevent accidents—and thus corroborating the impression, repeatedly expressed,—that

PREVENTION IS BETTER THAN CURE.

ADDITIONAL SUPPLEMENT.

IMPORTANT EXPERIMENT.

SINCE the publication of my Remarks on the Percussion Lock, many gentlemen have called on me, and various facts have been communicated, which have corroborated my opinion so fully, that my anxiety has been increased to prevent the danger arising from the bursting of gun-barrels. I considered it a public duty to put every gentleman on his guard; and, having done so, I am still bound to give the result of a new experiment, which has not only confirmed my fears, but I have no hesitation in adding, that for the future I shall never recommend the percussion lock with double barrels, without explaining to the purchaser the result of my experiments, and my conviction of the danger likely to arise from using them.

On the 19th of February, I proved a pair of double barrels on the percussion principle; and, although one pair had been proved at the Company of Gunmaker's proof-house, both in their single and double state—had stood the proof, and were marked as sound barrels—had been afterwards proved by me in the usual manner, both regular and water proof—yet when I proved them by the percussion principle, both barrels bulged, were much shivered—and were consequently spoiled.

The other pair had undergone the strictest proof at my PROOF-HOUSE—and such as would be generally considered sufficient to justify the strongest recommendation for safety — yet on trying them by the detonating principle, the result was the same—both barrels were seriously injured.

Feb. 22, 1823.—I have this day tried another pair of barrels, which had undergone the regular proof, and which I had absolutely fitted to the stock for sale, by specific order — both barrels failed.

Thus, for the purpose of satisfying numerous inquiries; for my own satisfaction; and on the principle of endeavouring to prevent the fatal accidents which are daily occurring, have I, at some expense, made these further trials—in the hope of conducing to perfection in the use of rifles and fowling pieces—but, above all, with an anxious desire to avert the dreadful calamities which may arise from pursuing a favourite recreation.

These barrels had stood every proof which is usually considered safe; and yet, from the suddenness with which the powder is ignited by the detonating principle, *all the barrels failed.* Consequently the result of these experiments convinces me, beyond any theoretical views entertained by others, that the proof of double barrels with the percussion locks *can only be satisfactorily proved by the detonating principle.* Every other proof, however it may appear to pass the ordeal of safety, is not a sufficient guarantee : and I can only add to my former injunctions, that no gentleman should venture to use the double barrel with the percussion lock, without having it first proved by its own strength and power.

July 14, 1823.—I printed the preceding Experiment on a separate slip of paper after the publication of the EIGHTH EDITION of this work; but my attention having been further called to this important subject in various ways, I am induced to reprint and attach it to the end of the volume; and at the same time to point out another great evil as well as danger in those double-barrelled guns, which have a much larger *elevating* top-piece or rib, as it is called, placed on the top of the barrels, than was formerly the practice; and which, instead of being an advantage is evidently the very reverse, as can be easily and satisfactorily explained. Previously to placing this rib, the barrels are made of equal thickness, and consequently when this *elevated* top-piece is added, one side of each barrel is thicker than the other; and it stands to reason, that, although the barrels may have been proved separately, and marked as sound, when this rib is added, the expansion of the barrel when fired cannot be equal, and, consequently, to use a homely phrase, " the weakest must go to the wall."

A barrel cannot be made too upright for service and safety—and I am decidedly of opinion, and I am borne out in the fact by various experiments, that the weight of the *elevated* top-piece or rib, more particularly in Percussion Guns, should be equally dispersed in the proper parts of the barrels, according to the old method, by which the barrels would not only become stronger and safer, but at the same time the sportsman would have. ▰▰ weight to carry.

FLINTS FOR MUSKETS.

The observation I made in p. 26, on the irregularity in the size of flints, particularly for muskets, induced me to try an experiment to obviate the evils so frequently complained of in the service. I therefore adopted a gauge, by which flints may be cut to one uniform and regular size ; and the Honorable Board of Ordnance and the East India Company have not only approved of the plan I submitted to their notice, but have given orders for gauges to be made for their use. The same gauge may be adapted to rifle guns, fusees, carbines, and pistols, and indeed to every description of fire arms : and must prove particularly advantageous where the jaws of the cocks are made right to receive them.

I have been accused of wishing to deteriorate the Percussion Lock altogether; and it has been asserted that I was interested in so doing. This is as untrue as it is unjust; and those who know me best will not attach so sordid and unworthy a motive to my anxiety for the public safety. I have shewn both the advantages and the disadvantages of the Percussion Lock; and although the latter predominate in a tenfold degree, as generally constituted, yet, by attending to the REQUISITE PROOF, (see p. 153,) and by correcting the errors I have pointed out, the double-barrelled fowling piece with the Percussion Lock, and every other, may be rendered perfectly safe; and will THEN become—what I have been most anxious to render every description of fire-arms—as free from danger as can be expected from the nature of all combustible materials.

That I am no enemy to improvement or invention, I think I have sufficiently proved—by those which I have myself introduced; and which have not only received general approbation, but for which the Society of Arts, &c. has awarded me three separate medals. This is the best refutation to the absurdity of the accusation. I have been too keen a sportsman myself to throw unnecessary obstacles in the " pursuit of game." I have pointed out errors—they may be corrected: I have proved that great danger exists—it may be surmounted. I have no ambition to gratify, and no object in view but the safety of my fellow countrymen. Let my motives then be fairly appreciated: and if, by a practical experience of nearly half a century, I should be the humble mean of averting one calamity— of preserving one life, invaluable to its family and connections—I may retire from the world with the consciousness of having performed an imperative duty.

6

At the request of many friends I am induced to add the following letter, from the Morning Post of Thursday, March 14, 1822, which, however complimentary it may be to me, contains truths so important, that I should be wanting in the duty I owe the public to withhold it. I therefore unhesitatingly comply with many sincere well-wishers, by re-publishing the letter, in the hope of averting those evils which it has been my study through a long life to point out and prevent.

IMPORTANT

IMPROVEMENT IN FIRE ARMS.

TO THE EDITOR.

SIR,

IT would be a melancholy detail to enumerate the various accidents that too frequently occur from the bursting of fire-arms; as also from the criminal negligence of those who keep them loaded without proper precautions of safety; from the insecure state of the arms themselves; and from that unaccountable propensity in some persons of pointing them at whoever may happen to be within reach. In a recent instance, an amiable young lady was sacrificed, and a most respectable family involved in misery, from a pistol having been incautiously placed in an infant's hand.*

As a Member of the Society of Arts, I have much pleasure in stating, that all these mischiefs

* See Morning Post, Jan. 3, 1822.

may be prevented by a simple and ingenious invention, which was submitted to the Society in 1810, and for which a Silver Medal was awarded to Mr. BAKER, of Whitechapel Road, Gunmaker to His MAJESTY. As the object of our Society is to encourage every thing that may tend to advance the progress of science, I feel called upon to draw your attention, and, through your extensively circulated Paper, that of the public, to this important invention; a general introduction of which would prevent many serious accidents, preserve many lives, and remove that dread which many people entertain from fire-arms—and justly so; as experience has too often fatally proved, that either curiosity or thoughtlessness has been the cause of those dreadful results which it has been your afflicting duty to communicate.*

Mr. BAKER's invention consists of a *safety-spring* to the lock, or *self-acting* bolt; the simplicity of which is perhaps its best recommendation; as, by the very motion of bringing the piece to the half-cock, the safety-spring is brought into action; and thus the possibility of its going off is

* In a Morning paper of this day, (July 9, 1823,) the following shocking accident is reported to have occurred at Tarvin:—" On Sunday, June 29, in the afternoon, a little girl about eight years old, only child of John Garnet, went into the house of a neighbour with a few cherries in her hand; when a boy about ten years old, taking up a gun in his hand, said he would shoot her if she would not give him some. Not knowing that the piece was loaded, he unfortunately pulled the trigger, when the contents were lodged in the poor child's head, and she instantly expired." This is another melancholy instance of the fatal effects of keeping fire-arms loaded without the necessary precautions."—E. B.

8

prevented : so that those who feel it necessary to keep arms constantly loaded may do so with perfect security, if they adopt this invaluable invention; which may also be easily applied to every lock, on whatever principle it may originally have been constructed.

This invention applies only to *prevent* fire-arms from being accidentally or incautiously discharged; but Mr. BAKER, for still further security, has also established a PROOF-HOUSE, at his Manufactory, under the patronage of His MAJESTY, where fowling-pieces and fire-arms of every description are submitted to a proof—first, by powder *the weight of the ball* (a practice of late years omitted by other gun-makers); and, secondly, by a *water-proof,* which will detect every flaw that may have escaped the first : and this double proof combined may then be considered a *perfect test of safety* from the bursting of barrels.

I have thus endeavored to point out a remedy for an acknowledged evil; and I cannot conclude without expressing my firm conviction, that, with these precautions, the sportsman may enjoy his recreation without fear, and that many valuable lives will be preserved both to their families and their country.

I have the honor to subscribe myself,

SIR,

Your obedient Servant,

PHILANTHROPOS.

March, 1822.

This Experiment was carried on by order of the HONORABLE BOARD OF ORDNANCE.
the 4th Day of February, 1800.

APPENDIX, N° I.

9 feet

This Barrel made by Mr. Baker two feet six in length, quarter turn in rifle was firmly fixed in a mortar bed as was all the other rifle barrels fixed on these experiments in such a manner as to be perfectly immoveable; 12 rounds were fired at a target 300 yards distance 11 of which struck as points here shewn the balls were the same that are used in mosquets, 14½ of which weigh a pound with four drams of powder; the balls were placed in a greased leather patch. After firing many foreign rifles as well as English, this had the preference of the whole.

Sign'd .... Thomas Bloomfield.
Colonel & Inspector of Royal Artillery

Woolwich, March 3, 1800.
APPENDIX, N° II. — *APPENDIX, N° III.*

This EXPERIMENT was by COMMAND of His PRESENT MAJESTY when PRINCE OF WALES June 4, 1803.

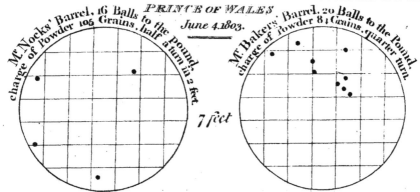

Mr Nock's Barrel, 16 Balls to the Pound, charge of Powder 105 Grains, half a turn in 2 feet.

Mr Baker's Barrel, 20 Balls to the Pound, charge of Powder 84 Grains, quarter turn.

7 feet

The two barrels 20 inches in length were fired at a target 200 yards distance, firmly fixed in a mortar bed in such a manner as to be perfectly immoveable; rounds from each barrel were fired, and points struck as in targets here shewn. Mr Baker's barrel was afterwards mounted in a stock & 18 rounds were fired by him from the shoulder, without a rest, at a target 100 yards distance with balls to the pound fixed to the cartridge as in use for smooth barrels; in rather less than seven minutes, 15 of which struck the target; the extreme divergence of the balls in inches is 22 to the right, 29½ to the left, 35½ over and 25 inches under.

Sign'd .... Benjamin Bloomfield.
Captain of the Royal Artillery & J. Miller
Colonel & Assistant Inspector of the Royal Artillery

Woolwich, 1803.

THE WEIGHT and DIAMETER of LEAD BALLS,

Cast from Moulds, One in the Pound to One Hundred in the Pound.

27½ Grains one Dram, 16 Drams one Ounce, 16 Ounces one Pound, Avoirdupoise.

DIVIDED IN 8 16 32 64 128 1024 PARTS OF
DITTO, AND IN 10 100 1000 PARTS OF } AN INCH,

by Ezekiel Baker.

1821.

Num of Balls	Ounces	Drams	Grains	100 Parts of Grain	Num of Balls	Inches	8	16	32	64	128	1024	Num of Balls	Inches	10	100	1000
1	16				1	1	5	1	1		2		1	1	6	7	
2	8				2	1	2	1				3	2	1	3	3	
3	5	5	9	12	3	1	1	-	1		1		3	1	1	6	
4	4				4	1		1				3	4	1		6	5
5	3	3	5	48	5		7	1	1	1		2	5		9	8	6
6	2	10	18	24	6		7		1	1		4	6		9	2	5
7	2	4	15	64	7		7				2	7	7		8	7	7
8	2				8		6	1		1	1	2	8		8	3	7
9	1	12	12	16	9		6		1	1		7	9		8		4
10	1	9	16	42	10		6			1	1	4	10		7	7	7
11	1	7	7	46	11		6					2	11		7	5	2
12	1	5	9	12	12		5	1	1			1 4	12		7	3	
13	1	3	18	94	13		5	1		1	1	1	13		7	1	2

R. Haseldine sculp. 7, Upper Rathbone Place.

Num. of Balls	Ounces	Drams	Grains	100 Parts of Grain	Num. of Balls	8	16	32	64	128	1024	Num. of Balls	10	100	1000
14	1	2	7	82	14	5	1				7	14	6	9	4
15	1	1	1	83	15	5		1	1		5	15	6	7	7
16	1				16	5		1			6	16	6	6	2
17		15	1	62	17	5			1		7	17	6	4	8
18		14	6	8	18	5				1	5	18	6	3	9
19		13	12	96	19	5					1	19	6	2	1
20		12	21	89	20	4	1	1	1		5	20	6	1	4
21		12	5	21	21	4	1	1		1	1	21	6		3
22		11	17	41	22	4	1	1			1	22	5	9	5
23		11	3	57	23	4	1		1	1		23	5	8	6
24		10	18	24	24	4	1			1	7	24	5	7	7
25		10	6	57	25	4	1			1		25	5	7	
26		9	23	15	26	4	1				2	26	5	6	5
27		9	13	17	27	4		1	1	1	1	27	5	6	5
28		9	3	91	28	4		1	1		1	28	5	4	8
29		8	22	64	29	4		1		1	4	29	5	4	3
30		8	14	59	30	4		1			6	30	5	3	7
31		8	7	6	31	4			1	1	7	31	5	3	
32		8			32	4			1	1	1	32	5	2	4
33		7	20	73	33	4			1		3	33	5	1	9
34		7	14	49	34	4				1	6	34	5	1	3
35		7	8	60	35	4				1	2	35	5	1	
36		7	3	4	36	4					5	36	5		5
37		6	25	14	37	3	1	1	1	1	6	37	4	9	8
38		6	20	16	38	3	1	1	1	1	1	38	4	9	3

Num. of Balls	Drams	Grains	100 Parts of Grain	Num. of Balls	8	16	32	64	128	1024	Num. of Balls	10	100	1000
39	6	15	43	39	3	1	1	1		5	39	4	8	9
40	6	10	95	40	3	1	1	1		2	40	4	8	6
41	6	6	67	41	3	1	1		1	5	41	4	8	2
42	6	2	61	42	3	1	1		1	3	42	4	8	
43	5	26	9	43	3	1	1		1		43	4	7	6
44	5	22	39	44	3	1	1			1	44	4	7	
45	5	18	85	45	3	1			1	7	45	4	6	8
46	5	15	47	46	3	1		1	1	2	46	4	6	3
47	5	12	23	47	3	1		1	1	1	47	4	6	2
48	5	9	12	48	3	1		1		7	48	4	6	
49	5	6	14	49	3	1		1		4	49	4	5	7
50	5	3	29	50	3	1			1	6	50	4	5	1
51	5		54	51	3	1			1	4	51	4	4	9
52	4	25	26	52	3	1			1	4	52	4	4	5
53	4	22	72	53	3	1				4	53	4	4	1
54	4	20	27	54	3	1				2	54	4	3	9
55	4	17	91	55	3		1	1	1	6	55	4	3	5
56	4	15	64	56	3		1	1		3	56	4	3	3
57	4	13	44	57	3		1	1	1		57	4	3	
58	4	11	32	58	3		1	1		6	58	4	2	8
59	4	9	28	59	3		1	1		5	59	4	2	7
60	4	7	30	60	3		1	1		3	60	4	2	5
61	4	5	38	61	3		1	1			61	4	2	2
62	4	3	53	62	3		1		1	6	62	4	2	
63	4	1	74	63	3		1		1	4	63	4	1	7

Num. of Balls	Drams	Grains	100 Parts of Grain	Num. of Balls	8	16	32	64	128	1024	Num. of Balls	10	100	1000
64	4			64	3		1		1	1	64	4	1	5
65	3	25	68	65	3		1			6	65	4	1	2
66	3	24	5	66	3		1			4	66	4	1	
67	3	22	46	67	3		1			2	67	4		8
68	3	20	93	68	3		1				68	4		6
69	3	19	43	69	3			1	1	6	69	4		4
70	3	17	98	70	3			1	1	3	70	4		2
71	3	16	57	71	3			1	1	1	71	4		
72	3	15	20	72	3			1	1		72	3	9	8
73	3	13	87	73	3			1		6	73	3	9	6
74	3	12	57	74	3	:		1		5	74	3	9	5
75	3	11	31	75	3			1		3	75	3	9	4
76	3	10	8	76	3			1		2	76	3	9	2
77	3	8	89	77	3				1	7	77	3	9	.
78	3	7	72	78	3				1	5	78	3	8	8
79	3	6	58	79	3				1	4	79	3	8	6
80	3	5	48	80	3				1	2	80	3	8	5
81	3	4	39	81	3					7	81	3	8	2
82	3	3	34	82	3					6	82	3	8	1
83	3	2	31	83	3		.			5	83	3	8	
84	3	1	31	84	3					4	84	3	7	9
85	3		33	85	3	:				2	85	3	7	7
86	2	26	73	86	3	:				1	86	3	7	6
87	2	25	79	87	2	1	1	1	1	5	87	3	7	2
88	2	24	88	88	2	1	1	1	1	4	88	3	7	1

Num. of Balls	Drams	Grains	100 Parts of Grain	Num. of Balls	8	16	32	64	128	1024	Num. of Balls	10	100	1000
89	2	23	98	89	2	1	1	1	1	2	89	3	6	9
90	2	23	11	90	2	1	1	1	1	1	90	3	6	8
91	2	22	25	91	2	1	1	1		6	91	3	6	6
92	2	21	42	92	2	1	1	1		5	92	3	6	5
93	2	20	60	93	2	1	1	1		4	93	3	6	4
94	2	19	80	94	2	1	1	1		3	94	3	6	3
95	2	19	1	95	2	1	1	1		2	95	3	6	2
96	2	18	24	96	2	1	1	1		1	96	3	6	1
97	2	17	49	97	2	1	1	1			97	3	6	
98	2	16	75	98	2	1	1		1	7	98	3	5	9
99	2	16	3	99	2	1	1		1	6	99	3	5	8
100	2	15	38	100	2	1	1		1	5	100	3	5	7

To ascertain what charge of powder and shot is right for all Guns, is not in my power, as there is so much variation in guns throwing their shot, altho' of the same dimensions in Bore, Length, Weight, &c, The charge is only to be obtaind by practice, as there is a certain charge that a gun will shoot with better than another, which is best ascertaind from the Sports in the Field; I have in general, found, two full drams, or two penny-weights and six grains, of good powder, to be equal to two ounces of shot, and one-third the weight of the Ball for a Rifle:

I have seen some Barrels shoot very well with equal measure of powder and shot, but it has been in general with Barrels of a full size Bore.

I have tryed waddings over the powder and shot of different sorts but have found none that equals the hat waddings for general perposes

Haselstine sculp.

Num.ᵣ of Shots.	In the Ounce.	8	16	32	64	128	1024	10	100	1000
Buck Shot Large.	5	3				1	5	3	8	8
Small Buck.	7	2	1	1	.		5	3	4	9
Grape for Musket.	9	2	1				6	3	1	8
Swan.	15	2			1		1	2	6	6
Goose.	24	1	1	1		1	5	2	3	1
Duck.	34	1	1		1		3	2		7
B.B.	50	1		1	1	1	4	1	8	3
B.	72	1		1			1	1	5	7
N.º1.	94	1			1	1	3	1	5	1
2	120	1				1	7	1	4	
3	140	1					2	1	2	7
4	175		1	1	1	1	5	1	2	2
5	240		1	1	1			1	1	8
6	260		1	1			3	1		1
7	320		1	1	1	1			9	9
8	622		1			1	6		7	6
9	900		1			1			7	
10	1600		1				1		6	3
Dust.	4300			1	1	1	3		5	

*The Quantity of small Shots in one Ounce, and the
Diameter of them in Eighth and Tenth parts of an Inch.
The Shots are different of the sundry Manufacturers;
and vary in size, I have taken the average of three of
them, and find them as above stated.*

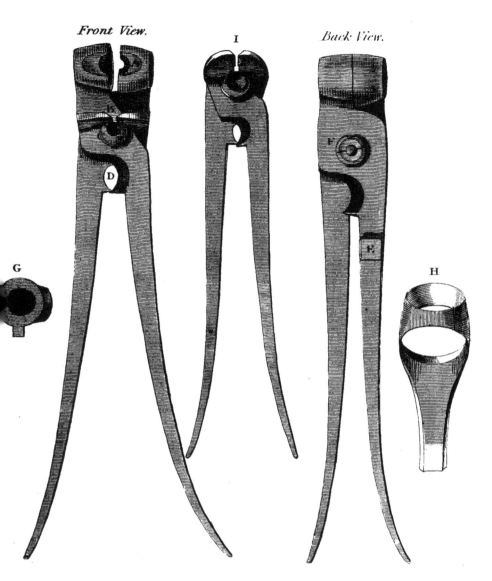

The explanation of the Bullet Moulds.

A. The Countersink, the Lead is pored in the mould to form the Ball.
B. The Cutter that cuts the ball from the neck.
C. The Cup the ball is laid in to be cut off.
D. The Cutter in the old way by cutting off a ball will shew the advantage of the new one.
E. A solid piece attached to the mould to screw in a vice to cut off the balls when oppertunity offers.
F. A screw that screws the revit in the moulds.
G. The inside of the mould.
H. A Punch to cut patches for Rifle Balls.
I. A Pair of Nippers without moulds to cut off Balls.

Milton Keynes UK
Ingram Content Group UK Ltd.
UKHW021447250824
447315UK00007B/42